Henry Zirndorf

Some jewish women

Henry Zirndorf

Some jewish women

ISBN/EAN: 9783743310469

Manufactured in Europe, USA, Canada, Australia, Japa

Cover: Foto ©Lupo / pixelio.de

Manufactured and distributed by brebook publishing software (www.brebook.com)

Henry Zirndorf

Some jewish women

Some Jewish Women

BY

Henry Zirndorf.

Translated from the German.

Philadelphia:
THE JEWISH PUBLICATION SOCIETY OF AMERICA
1892.

COPYRIGHT, 1892.
BY THE JEWISH PUBLICATION SOCIETY OF AMERICA.

PRESS OF
EDWARD STERN & CO.
PHILADELPHIA.

TO THE MEMORY

OF MY DAUGHTER,

EMILIE ESTHER ZIRNDORF,

WHO DEPARTED THIS LIFE IN

DETROIT, APRIL 23, 1882,

These Sketches of Notable Womanhood are inscribed in undying tenderness.

PREFACE.

WHEN, sometime ago, I undertook to present an historic delineation of the women of Judaism, I was led to think that it would be better to adopt a method of treatment different from that of previous writers on the subject. After some hesitation, therefore, I concluded to arrange my material in the form of a series of biographies, this arrangement being best adapted for emphasizing alike both the bright and dark sides of the lives to be presented.

Mankind, in general, seems to show itself in the most favorable light when sustained, in suffering, by some degree of intellectual power; and to this rule woman forms no exception. The Talmudic period, however, so far as concerns women, is, perhaps, the richest within the entire domain of history. In this epoch, with its great Hadrianic persecution and the several lesser ones, in this age of a nation's sorrow and of harsh reality, the enamored maiden and the matron, the simple housewife and the spoiled, peevish sultana of the middle classes, the modest helpmeet, and the heroic sufferer, all stand out as prominently as one could wish for the purpose of description; while all the needful humor is supplied by the shrew and the Xanthippe.

The Talmudic group of women provides, if not a greater at least as great, a wealth of material as the Biblical. For, in lieu of the prophetesses, the Talmud gives us women of true prophetic insight and of mental greatness; as, for example, the wise Beruria, Akiba's wife, Rabbi Ishmael's mother, and others. Yet the style employed by the Talmud in writing history is often obscure and difficult, and Talmudic literature, as a primary source, presents obstacles for the literary worker which only the most patient care can overcome. Any presentation of such a subject, must, above all, aim at completeness, and it is often necessary to fill out the groundwork of the picture by drawing on our general knowledge of the particular time and localities treated. Neither the smallest note nor the slightest variation in the text must be passed over as unessential.

When, accordingly, I received the flattering invitation to issue, in an English translation, some of my sketches of Jewish women contributed to *The Deborah*,* I was easily persuaded, for the reasons already given, to take up the Talmudic period and the closely related epochs.

The reader will readily perceive that here, as in other periods of history, the material is not evenly distributed. There are times so full of strife and human distress, that woman and the domestic world are hardly mentioned at all. Foremost among these are the early Maccabean wars, during which period there is seldom any reference to women. From the apocryphal Scriptures I could gather only enough material for the sketches of Judith and the Mother of the

---

* A weekly journal published in Cincinnati.

Seven Martyrs, and both of these belong to legend rather than to history.

In the succeeding period—the Græco-Roman—the conditions are more favorable. Salome Alexandra, Mariamne, and Berenice are characters whose good and bad qualities alike might justly engage the pen of a Plutarch. I have not, of course, presumed to undertake so difficult a task. Although I have not shirked critical investigation and careful research, I shall be amply content with the assurance of having gathered available material for a future history of women.

I may say, in conclusion, that it is my intention, at some future day, to add to this collection the portraits of the women of the time of the Gaonim and of the Middle Ages.

THE AUTHOR.

Cincinnati, October, 1892.

CONTENTS.

Preface, ... v

FROM THE APOCRYPHA:
Judith, ... 5
The Mother of the Seven Martyrs, ... 15

THE GRÆCO-ROMAN PERIOD:
Queen Salome Alexandra, ... 27
Mariamne, the Hasmonean, ... 55
Helena, Queen and Proselyte, ... 83
Berenice, ... 106

THE TALMUDIC AGE:
Martha, Daughter of Boëthus, ... 121
Ima Shalom, ... 139
Rachel, Rabbi Akiba's Wife, ... 152
Beruria, ... 162
Rabbi Meïr's Pupil, ... 174
Rabbi Ishmael's Mother, ... 184
Rabbi Judah's Maid-Servant, ... 193
The Married Couple of Sidon. (An Apologue), . 205
A Group of Xanthippes, ... 215
Jalta, ... 223
Abaji's Foster-Mother, ... 233
The Two Chomas, ... 243
Weasel and Well as Witnesses, ... 253
Conclusion, ... 268

A

FROM

THE APOCRYPHA.

I.

JUDITH.

Not long after the return of the Jews from the Babylonian exile, Nebuchadnezzar—who, strangely enough, is assumed in the book of Judith to be still living,* and appears there by way of variety, as king of Assyria,† instead of king of Babylonia—is reported to have despatched his general Holofernes to the western and southern parts of Upper Asia, to subdue several of the nations that began to waver in their loyalty. On this expedition the Assyrian

---

* He died in 561 B.C. Of the Israelites it is said: "For they had but newly (*i. e.*, in 536) marched up out of the captivity." Judith, IV, 3. This completely subverts chronology.

† This designation cannot be allowed even as a mere title; for when Assyria (606) fell a prey to the allied powers of Media and Babylonia, it was the former state that took the main province, Assyria proper, as its share. G. Rawlinson, *The Seven Great Monarchies*, II, 239.

army came into the vicinity of Bethulia or Bethylua, a strong fortification in northern Palestine, which neither history nor geography has been able to locate up to the present time. Irritated by the vigilance of the Judeans, who were equipped for defence, Holofernes prepared, by closely investing it and cutting off the supply of water, to compel the city to surrender. While the elders were considering the advisability of submitting to the barbarous victor, a valiant woman, on the other hand, was revolving the design of freeing her fellow-citizens from the impending horrors of war.

It was Judith, a beautiful widow of rank. Ever since her husband's death she had been leading a life of austerity, even imposing upon herself prolonged fasts; but, moved by the general distress, she now emerged with manly daring from her seclusion.

For the first time in three years she laid aside the dark veil of mourning, bathed and anointed herself with the fragrant spices of the East, arranged her hair in neat braids beneath her becoming head-band, and wrapped her charming form once again in gay, magnificent robes, so long neglected. Her adornment was in every way complete; the sandals on her feet, her bracelets, the clasps on her shoulders, her ear-rings, rings, and many other ornaments, all shone brightly, as in the happy days when Menasseh, her beloved husband, was yet alive.

"She made herself very beautiful to ensnare the eyes of men." X, 4.

After these preparations and one of those long and fervent prayers, in which apocryphal literature abounds, Menasseh's charming widow, attended by her maid, left the city and turned her steps directly to Holofernes' tent in the Assyrian camp. The general's pride was flattered by her wily words, while her whole appearance captivated his senses. At night, in his tent, she lulled him into a deep slumber with brimming goblets of wine. Then, with his own sword, she cut off his head and carried it back with her, as a bloody trophy, to the city. The Assyrians, deprived of their commander, were seized with a panic and fled, just as the hordes of Sennacherib did on a former occasion; and thus the city of Bethulia was delivered from all fear of the enemy.

This picture, by no means well conceived, gives evidence neither of wealth of imagination nor refinement of taste; nevertheless it is of interest for our collection of female portraits, in so far as it shows what the poetry of that age, influenced as it was by current opinion, regarded as the possible attributes of a patriotic woman. And we are at once impressed with the fact that we are dealing with a period of great excitement, which permitted love of country to manifest itself only in wild excesses, subverted all morality and sense of right, and stripped even female nature of its noblest characteristics.

"Its [the whole book's] moral principle," very aptly says Dr. Wise, "eulogizing an assassin, is low, and points to a time of hostility and fanaticism."*

---

* I. M. Wise, *History of the Hebrews' Second Commonwealth*, p. 128.

There is but *one* period in all the history of Judaism, in which there was the concurrence of circumstances necessary to bring about this state of feeling. I have reference to the time of the struggle against Antiochus Epiphanes. Hence Hugo Grotius was right when he assigned the composition of the book of Judith to the period of the Syrian disturbances, and made the ethical-religious principle of strengthening the Israelites in their hope of victory its underlying basis.* But it is a pity that Grotius weakened his hypothesis by an extremely finespun allegory. Judith is said to represent the Jewish nation, Bethulia the Temple of Jerusalem, Assyria the arrogance of the enemy, Nebuchadnezzar is Satan, and to Holofernes is awarded the distinction of being נחש הלפר, *i. e.*, the beadle of the serpent or demon, and in this form represents the hated Antiochus. Now there is in Chaldaic an expression לופר, meaning *catch-poll, bea-*

---

* *Ut Judæi spe divinæ liberationis confirmarentur*, Commentar. ad Judith.

dle,* but nothing can be done with the ה which occurs in the word, and indeed the whole designation is both an anachronism and un-Jewish.

Moreover, the explanation is not so far to seek, and there is no need to resort to such allegorical ingenuities. During the persecution under Antiochus, it must not be forgotten, Jewish patriots ran great risks in candidly avowing their opinions concerning the severe oppression which Israel endured. It had to be done *sub rosa*, that is, in the guise of poetry; and doubtless it was at this time that some enthusiastic Chasid gave the story of Judith to the nation. His object was unmistakable; this was his way of exclaiming to his co-religionists: "Behold! a weak woman is not incapable of such a deed! Will you men shrink from the attempt? Will you suffer yourselves to be butchered unresistingly by the Syrians, to be betrayed by the Hellenists in your midst?"

---

* Genes. Rabba, 61 ; Levy, *Neuhebr. und Chaldäisch. Wörterbuch*, II, 490.

Judith.

The author of this fiction, as already observed, was no genius at poetical invention. Two of the principal features of the production are mere reminiscences from the earlier Scriptures. The slaying of a sleeping man is a repetition of the act of Jael,* and the flight of the Assyrian army is a somewhat more elaborated copy of the flight of Sennacherib and his host.† It is only in his constant emphasis of Chasidaic rigor, in his preference for mortifications of the flesh, abstinence, fasting, long prayers and similar asceticism, that the unknown author has shown some originality. Of the three hundred and forty verses of the little book I have counted exactly ninety-one, including the prayers, which advocate a truly fanatical abstinence and which could have been written only by a Chasid of that agitated epoch. This peculiarity, to which critics have hitherto paid no attention, is, however,

---

* Judges, IV, 21.

† 2 Kings, XIX, 35; Isaiah, XXXVII, 36; 2 Chronicles, XXXII, 21.

not unimportant for a proper estimate of the little epic. Above all, the date of composition can thus be fixed with precision. The legend of Judith owes its origin, as already indicated, to the years of strife and suffering from 170 to 166.

If we ask whether the Chasid poet succeeded in arousing the Jewish spirit, as he intended, history answers with a significant No. Besides, the native sense of truth, characteristic of the Jewish mind, demands even of poetry a larger measure of reality. It is on this account that the Jewish consciousness has always turned with a sort of repugnance from the story of Judith; for it contains hardly a word of truth. Josephus knows nothing of the book of Judith, or perhaps pretends to know nothing; the Talmud has no knowledge of it, and two Midrashic adaptations, which Jellinek has incorporated into his *Beth-Hamidrash*,* manifestly belong to a rather late period. The very name Judith was only used in a later

---

* Books I and II.

age in naming girls, being scarcely ever employed in the earlier rabbinical centuries.

All the more kind, on the other hand, was the reception accorded the book of Judith by the Christian church. Clemens of Rome, one of the earliest Fathers of the Church,— he died in the year 100—mentions the work; Jerome made a thorough study of it; and the Council of Trent, at its fourth session, went to the extent of awarding it the full honors of canonicity.

As to the heroine of this apocryphal book, she has been especially favored by painters. Few subjects have so often been treated on canvas as Menasseh's enticing widow. Still the manner of treatment, for the most part sensational and grossly realistic, is not exactly calculated to gain her sympathetic friends. So far as I am personally concerned, whenever I have visited a picture gallery I sought to avoid the avenging beauty. This, however, is next to impossible in the galleries of Europe, where pictures of Judith of all styles fairly jostle one another. Indeed, at every turn you are sure to behold this beautiful, terrible woman, with her purple sandals, her diadem, her golden bracelets, her eyes that draw forth your very soul, and, hanging at her side, not the beaded purse and the *bonbonnière*, but—O how horrible!—the bloody Gorgon head of the enemy.

II.

THE MOTHER OF THE SEVEN MARTYRS.

OF the many tragic scenes which owe their origin to the cruelty of Antiochus Epiphanes one especially, by reason of its attendant circumstances, has deeply impressed itself on the memory of posterity. I refer to the martyrdom of a Jewish mother and her seven heroic sons, as related in the harrowing account that has come down to us. Despite the edict of the Syrian despot, a large number of Jews remained true to the religion of their fathers. Among these were seven brothers, who, with their mother, were accordingly seized and brought before the king. The historical part of this story we must assign to the year 167–166 B.C., a period of much suffering; and it is not at all improbable that the scene of the dismal event was Antioch, the Syrian capital, where many a distinguished victim of those cruel times met his fate.

By divers threats and atrocities these eight innocent beings were to be forced to eat swine's flesh: in other words, to join in the worship of the goddess Demeter, to whom the pig was sacred. But, resisting pressure and coercion, they refused to the bitter end and perished one after another amid unheard-of tortures, yet full of high-souled contempt for the tyrant and with the enthusiastic confession of their faith on their dying lips.

Such is the account given by Jason of Cyrene, as we find it in the seventh chapter of the Second Book of Maccabees. He is otherwise unknown as a historian, having flourished in an age of which we have very scanty records. The book ascribed to Josephus, however, and known by the name of "The Fourth Book of Maccabees, or Upon the Supremacy of Reason," has treated this remarkable subject in greater detail. Notwithstanding its too elaborate embellishments, in the Græco-Alexandrian style, the unknown rhetorician has given us a narrative of a truly elevating character. From the Hebrew-Greek cycle of legends this story of tears and bloodshed found its way into Talmudical literature; and it is a peculiar circumstance, worthy of note, that the two best known and most detailed narratives from Talmudical sources place the event in the Hadrianic period of persecution.* For my own part, I conclude from this fact that the story, in its main features, is not entirely without historical value, in spite of its traditional trappings. A thoroughly mythical story could accommodate itself only with difficulty to such usage, while the reverse might easily be the case with a tradition based upon more or less distinct recollections of the popular memory. Most of the speeches attributed to these hapless youths, as well as many other rhetorical and Hagadic embellishments, are, doubtless, later accretions. As such, they are of course to be rejected, while the event itself must be

---

* Gittin 57b; Echa Rabbathi on Echa, 1, 16.

reduced to its true historical proportions. But, this process of elimination once completed, there can no longer be any good reason for discrediting what remains. Scenes of torture and murder such as the one here described must have been plentiful, as, indeed, martyrs were common in the days of the cruel Seleucidæ.

This fearless woman, whose name is not found in the earlier sources, is by the concurrence of the Hagadic records of a later date now commonly called *Hannah*, although the Echa-Midrash speaks only of a *Miriam*, daughter of the baker Boëthus. But Miriam or Hannah—the name is immaterial—fully merits the distinction of a place among the noblest of her sex, and must be mentioned in any enumeration of prominent Israelitish women. For, even if her right to pass for a historical personage be disputed, even if the hazardous attempt to relegate her entirely to the realm of fiction were successful, yet she belongs by inseparable ties to universal literature and, by the legendary use which has been made of the character, poetry and rhetoric unite, as it were, in declaring a Jewish woman quite capable of such a sacrifice.

It is not necessary to dwell here on the pathetic incidents of this story. Everybody knows them either from the original account or one of the many subsequent narratives; nor, in view of the difficulty of the attempt to discriminate between history and fiction, would it be worth the trouble to examine into the local conditions and circumstances of the different versions. The afflicted mother, who, according to the Talmud, rivals Abraham in the magnitude of her sacrifice to the Deity, has not, indeed, received from art the kindly treatment given to other sorrowing women; but poetry, on the other hand, has taken the sufferer to her heart and invested her with a full measure of glory. And we may say that the martyred mother, reposing in an unknown grave, gradually grew into a poetic character; new refulgence has been shed upon her, a fresh flower added to her wreath, by each succeeding literary production, until now this heroine is associated in our minds with the steadfast faith that knows no fear of death. Neither in history nor in the creations of genius can we find a more effective picture of piety embracing death in all its forms. This noble woman's heroism has, however, a deeper significance, when thought of in connection with the new period of splendor which the Maccabean victories secured to the religious life of Israel in the years that immediately followed. It cannot be denied that martyrs, as a rule, do not appear to advantage by the side of conquering heroes; but here it is otherwise: the martyred mother makes quite as strong an impression upon us as the victorious Hasmonean. Indelibly stamped on the history of the times as are the triumphs of this illustrious priestly family, yet their good fortune is but transitory; and we feel instinctively that Israel's brightest hopes, as well as its richest spiritual treasures, lie stored with the noble, loyal dead—the sacrificed Chasidim.

On the whole, this was a most extraordinary age, reckless in warfare, daring in conquest, eager to brave suffering and death. Here we have a resolute, heroic woman, who, in the words of the unknown panegyrist: "With spirit hard as adamant, leading on that number of sons to immortality, adjures them to die for the faith."* Then again we see the hoary priest Mattathias and his five warlike sons, not one of whom was destined to die a peaceful death. Surely the picture of this great epoch is incomplete without the woman who, as wife, widow, and aged matron, presents the most striking example of contrasted weakness and strength to be found in the literature of mankind.

And shall not I, too, add some slight token of my veneration for this heroine of legend and history? What classic pens have written of her is known sufficiently; but before me lies the book "*Anaf ez abot*,"† by Baruch Schoenfeld, a talented Hebrew

---

* Fourth Book of Maccabees, 16.

† Buda, 1841.

poet of recent times, and I find there a poem instinct with deep feeling. It is entitled, "Miriam and Her Sons." I have made a free translation of its concluding stanzas in the belief that, in thus honoring the subject of this brief sketch, I am at the same time contributing something to a better appreciation of a writer whose name I would fain preserve from unmerited oblivion.

" With bland, dissembling speech the king conceals
    The rage that burns within his savage breast ;
Yet son and mother steadfast still remain :
    Much have they borne, and now will bear the rest.
And Miriam cries : ' Let venomed flattery
    Not lead, O son, thy guileless mind astray !
Think on thy brethren, in their bloom that died,
    Lest God and race they basely might betray.
As angels pure, they at the throne of heaven
    Now sound their harps to the Eternal One ;
Wouldst thou rejoin that blessed band, no path
    Save that of blood will lead thee there, my son !

" Hodaia, noble offspring ! He quails not,
    Upon his childlike features plays a smile.
Haste thee, blaspheming tyrant ! See, I scorn
    Thee and thy fury, scorn each spiteful wile.

My God still lives, from Him come weal and woe,
    But Zeus and Ares are a mockery.
Set free anon, transfigured, in bright realms
    We twain soon with our fathers' God shall be.
There days of darkness no more we behold,
    Nor hear the sentence that once terrified ;
And raptures, to the earthly sense denied,
    And songs of seraphim shall welcome us
To Eden's groves, who for the faith have died."

THE

GRÆCO-ROMAN

PERIOD.

III.

QUEEN SALOME ALEXANDRA.

THE Maccabean age, whose fierce combats and constant excitement gave a touch of passion even to piety, was on the whole not very favorable to the development of female genius. The period was one propitious to warfare, to the growth of new ideas, and to those measures generally in which the influence of men greatly predominates, and consequently women had very little opportunity to distinguish themselves. For nearly two entire generations, during which the Hasmonean dynasty took the lead in public affairs, they played such an insignificant part in the important events of the time as the brevity of ancient historians would scarcely permit them to notice; but then, at last, a woman appeared who, by reason of her great abilities, held undisputed sway for a long time.

Salome Alexandra, the first to bear the

name of queen under the new order of things, twice as consort and once in her own right as dowager, is also the woman in Jewish history who has won renown in this exalted station through her noble qualities, her talents, and her rare achievements. This lofty historical character, known in Talmudical literature as Salominon or Salomita שלכיתו,* was born toward the year 143 B.C., about the time when the noble Jonathan lost his life by Trypho's treachery. History tells us nothing of her ancestry or birthplace; but from the fact that Simon ben-Shetach, president of the Sanhedrin, was her brother, and also from her early alliance with the Hasmoneans, it is probable that she was a native of Jerusalem. The latter fact leads me to conclude that she belonged to a family of the Aaronic line; for the early members of the aspiring Hasmonean house moved in a circle com-

---

* Kohelet, Rabba on 7, 11; Sabbat 16b; Graetz, *Geschichte der Juden*, Vol. III, p. 530, makes a happy emendation.

posed exclusively of Chasidim, and were no doubt influenced by policy and family tradition to prefer their own relatives in their choice of consorts. Furthermore, the interest which her brother, who was well versed in the Scriptures, took in the nazaritic sacrifices, makes it more than credible that he was connected with the priesthood.

However this may be, the noble Jewish maiden, precocious as she was, soon became a pet in the house of John Hyrcanus, and in due time was betrothed to that ruler's eldest son, Judah Aristobulus. Her spouse inherited the brilliant rather than good qualities of his glorious father: his ambition and martial spirit without his prudence and circumspection, his Saducean proclivities without his patriotism and sympathy for the people. Salome, on the other hand, was thoroughly imbued with the true spirit of the Chasidim; but, though she guarded her ideals sacredly, she had early learned the art of self-control and the value of secrecy. So long as Judah Aristobulus lived under his father's government, this marriage would seem to have been a happy one. His young wife enthusiastically seconded the aims of the newly formed Pharisaic party; she was proud of her brother, the foremost scribe of his day; she cherished the hope, perhaps, of eventually turning her husband's unbridled love of conquest to some noble purpose. John Hyrcanus having passed away about the year 107, after a long life, Judah's ambition to ascend the throne, a distinction for which he had been secretly longing, was finally realized. At this time Salome had attained her thirty-sixth year, and, as Judah Aristobulus was considerably older than his four brothers, she must in all probability have been married to him twenty years. She was now styled queen; for Aristobulus (this name he took out of love for the Greeks) was the first to place the diadem upon his head.* Did this honor bring her happiness? Far from it. Though she kept her anxiety locked within her own breast, she was concerned about the future.

---

* Josephus, Antiquities, XIII, 11, I.

The year that followed was a turbulent and disastrous one, and Salome had many and various troubles to contend against. Though peaceful relations still existed between the royal house and the popular party, signs of a rupture were not wanting; the disturbing influence of coming events was at work. What is now to be related has been preserved by tradition in the form of stories, more or less fanciful, but the real facts are by no means beyond recognition. The new king imprisoned his aged mother, in order to deprive her of the right to act as co-regent—a power conferred on her by the last will of John Hyrcanus. My pen shrinks from repeating the further charge made by Josephus, who holds Judah responsible for the starvation of his mother; indeed, this statement is regarded by recent writers as an exaggeration.* There is no doubt, however, that he kept three of his brothers in a gloomy dungeon during his brief reign. For his remaining brother—the brilliant, but thoughtless

---

* See Graetz and Wise.

and unruly Antigonus—he retained a certain fondness. But his morbid envy and the tattle of courtiers soon disturbed even these friendly relations. While on a march of conquest, the glory of which Antigonus shared with him, Judah was seized with an insidious disease, which necessitated his return to Jerusalem, and to his younger brother was therefore entrusted the work of completing his interrupted victory. This circumstance it was which seems to have first kindled the irascible Judah's wrath against the unfortunate prince. When, shortly after, Antigonus led the army back to the capital, the enemies of the victorious general easily persuaded the king that he had a most dangerous foe in his brother, and the latter, ignorant of the designs on his life, was accordingly despatched by the guards in that part of the palace called Strato's Tower.

Tradition has connected Antigonus' unhappy fate with all the superstitions and delusions of that age, and Josephus even goes to the length of charging the queen with complicity in the cruel deed. He tells us that, by a treacherous message of hers, the hapless Antigonus was betrayed into the hands of his assassins.* So grave an accusation is worthy of the attention of history only when supported by strong internal evidence; in the absence of such evidence, the accused, in this as in all similar cases, is entitled to be entirely exonerated. A woman whose character was in all other respects above reproach ought not to be thus lightly convicted of participation in so terrible a crime. Such a verdict bears on its face the stamp of silly credulity. So far as we can judge, the queen had nothing to gain by her brother-in-law's death; and simply to assume that she was actuated by hatred, without any assignable reason, is wholly unjustifiable under the circumstances. Of the two brothers next entitled to the throne, Antigonus and Alexander, the former was by far the more brilliant. Moreover, Josephus, who is alone responsible for

---

* Antiquities, XIII, 11, 2.

c

this aspersion against the noble queen, has otherwise shown himself so unfair in his estimate of her—a matter about which I shall have a word to say later on—that we are hardly warranted in putting any faith in his assertion. At all events, our classical historian certainly lived in an age so far removed from the period in which the events described took place, that his narrative could have been based only on unsafe traditions, colored by the bitter animosities of party strife. When political parties attempt to write history, they are only too apt to see crimes in each other's successes, and this, no doubt, explains how the crowned widow, who was guilty of nothing more than a somewhat too hasty marriage with the passionate Jannæus, came to be regarded by posterity as the mortal enemy of the murdered Antigonus. It is quite possible, too, that even before the latter's death, slanderous tongues may have whispered their base suspicions of a guilty passion between Salome and Alexander.

Judah Aristobulus survived Antigonus

only a few hours, dying amid agonies of body and soul to which he gave vent in violent self-accusations. Salome Alexandra, however, was not the woman to waste time in idle grief. She had a great wrong to repair—the imprisonment of her three brothers-in-law; and no sooner had her husband closed his eyes than she released the captives. At this time, 106 B.C., the widowed queen was the most resolute and courageous of the Hasmonean line, and on her energy this bold, proud family was solely dependent for its continuance in power. To the eldest of the liberated brothers, Alexander, she offered her hand and the crown; the second, Absalom, stood in such subordinate relations to the throne that we hear nothing more of him until he is referred to as the father-in-law of Aristobulus II; the name of the third, history has entirely forgotten. Perhaps he is the same person whom Josephus mentions as having been assassinated by his brother Jannæus.[*]

---

[*] Antiquities, XIII, 12, 1.

This marriage of the mature widow, thirty-seven years of age, with Alexander, a young man of but twenty-three, whose surname appears in Josephus as Jannæus, in the Talmud as Jannai, has given rise to considerable dispute among historians; yet few facts in history are better established. As high-priest, it is urged, Jannai could not possibly have married a widow; he was even (Sanhedrin II, 1), expressly exempted from the Levirate marriage. Hence, Graetz very strangely concludes that Salome's marriage to Aristobulus must have been a mere invention, and that Alexander was the queen's first husband.* But, in adopting this view, he introduces another improbability even more difficult of explanation. Either he assumes that this unequal marriage took place, without assigning the slightest reason why a woman of thirty-seven should marry a young man of twenty-three, or he is compelled to show that Salome was not so old by at least fifteen

---

* *Geschichte der Juden*, Vol. III, p. 128.

years as she is said to have been when Aristobulus died. He makes no such attempt, however,* and, in view of the many events in which she had hitherto been concerned, it would have been quite futile.

Only two solutions of this difficulty are conceivable. The marriage may have taken place before Jannai was appointed high-priest. Cases of this kind are, indeed, minutely provided for in the Halacha. "If," says the Mishnah, "he is appointed high-priest after he has been betrothed to a widow, he may contract marriage with her. This actually happened in the case of Joshua ben-Gamala; he married the widow Martha, daughter of Boëthus, and afterwards the king appointed him high-priest."† But it is a still more plausible supposition that, at this early period, very little importance was attached to such legal subtleties. Without giving the matter much thought, Jannai simply married his sister-in-law, and

---

* *Geschichte der Juden*, Vol. III, p. 155.

† Jebamoth, 6, 4.

together they assumed the royal power which his ambition had coveted. Both being persons of rank and influence, no authoritative protest was made against their resolution. There is another important circumstance in support of this opinion. History strangely omits all reference to Alexander's labors as high-priest, and in the Talmud* only indirect mention is made of the fact of his having held such an office. It is just possible, too, that there was a provision for allowing substitutes in such cases.

Salome Alexandra entered into this new union with all the tact and prudence of a great woman. What was it that united two such dissimilar natures? Was it love, worldly advantage, or political considerations? A difficult question—which the historian may not leave entirely unanswered. From a knowledge of Alexander's character we are forced to the conclusion that he could neither understand nor appre-

---

* Sota 48a.

ciate such a woman as Salome Alexandra. This prince gave the reins to the basest passions. Deceitful, cruel, possessed of the revengeful instincts of a brute, he was, at the same time, dominated by insatiable ambition. He was addicted to drink and, as we know from Josephus,* led in other respects a very dissolute life. In him we see to how great an extent the Maccabean race had already degenerated; military valor was the only one of all the Hasmonean virtues which he still retained. And this was the man to whom Salome, with all her clearness of vision and penetration of mind, entrusted herself for twenty-seven years. Bearing him two children, enduring his many vices, having but little sympathy for his ambitious projects, she sat patiently on the throne which her cautious prudence had helped to secure, perfectly resigned to her lot. Nay, she really seems to have loved this inordinately passionate man with all the tender affection which women, and

---

* Antiquities, XIII, 14, 2.

in fact human beings generally, lavish on those for whose happiness and elevation they have labored most zealously. Before his baser self had gained complete mastery over Alexander, this experienced woman exercised a decided influence upon him. More than once, without his knowing it, she led her impetuous husband with a firm hand from the path of error and restrained him from acting rashly.

For a proper appreciation of this important period of the royal lady's life, it is far more essential to know her attitude toward the leading Jewish factions than to study the many wars in which Alexander Jannai was involved. These bitter strifes followed one another in swift succession, and rarely left any opportunity for an interval of peace. During fully nineteen years of this turbulent reign there was an almost uninterrupted series of battles, victories and defeats; and in these hot contests, many of which were acts of revenge, the strength of the royal zealot spent itself long before its time. The seizure of the maritime towns led to a four years' war with Ptolemy Soter (105-101), ending with Jannai's defeat by Theodorus, prince of Philadelphia; but in a campaign of two years' duration (99-97) the Jewish king fully retrieved his losses, regaining possession of the seaports by a barbarous act of revenge. The Arabian war (94-92) lasted more than two years, and the ignominious retreat before the victorious hosts of Obedas, by which Jannai was obliged to terminate this struggle, inspired his Pharisaic enemies at home with the courage to undertake the disastrous war against him which, continuing from 92 to 86 B.C., ended with the infamous battle of Bethome. On that day Alexander, who, with the introduction of foreign mercenaries, resorted to hideous forms of cruelty altogether alien to the Jewish race, had eight hundred captured Pharisees nailed to the cross amid the most revolting circumstances. The years from 84 to 81 were taken up with his conquests in the northeast, and even in the last year of his life (79) we see this restless warrior laying siege to Ragaba. His life offers a noteworthy example of undeserved good fortune; for, in spite of his repeated and disastrous defeats, in spite of his clumsy and expensive methods of warfare, and in spite of his political hypocrisy, he bequeathed to his successor a kingdom which, considerably enlarged, commanded great respect.

The wise, pious queen witnessed these successes and reverses, for the most part without much show of interest. She directed her attention to matters which, as she judged, were of far greater importance to the welfare of the state, namely, the internal administration of affairs. For eleven years she had managed to keep the king on good terms with the Pharisaic party, who represented the best element of the nation. Historians must be very short-sighted, when such truths escape their attention. Everything, indeed, points to this explanation as the correct view of Salome's policy; the aged Hyrcanus had gone over to the Sadducees; Judah Aristobulus had administered the government, during his brief reign, in the Sadducean spirit; in fact, Sadducean tendencies floated in the air. The outlook for this proud and aggressive party was most favorable; even the Sanhedrin had a Sadducean majority.

Yet the great body of the people was Pharisaic at heart, their piety was tinctured with Phariseeism, and in these times of trouble the popular spirit derived comfort from the law and ancestral customs. This haughty prince, therefore, who permitted nothing to stand in the way of his wishes, was careful to spare the people's feelings. He was not, indeed, drawn toward Phariseeism; but he nevertheless tried to preserve a becoming attitude of impartiality, taking pains not to offend that very vigilant party. This continued for the space of eleven years. By what device of female wisdom was Salome Alexandra enabled to bring about this good understanding? For no one will doubt that the honor belongs exclusively to her. When she offered Alexander her hand in marriage, thereby paving his way to the throne, did she exact of him a solemn promise to spare the Pharisees? By no means. The explanation is much simpler. The queen was herself an enthusiastic Pharisee, and, above all, taught by example. It was this knowledge of her friendly feelings in regard to them which, beyond a doubt, made the Pharisaic party prudent and loyal in their conduct toward the court.

On the fatal Feast of Tabernacles of the year 95, however, these peaceful relations unfortunately came to an end. Inflated with angry pride, the king, instead of emptying the cup of water into the golden horns of the altar, poured the contents on the ground, in contemptuous derision of the Pharisaic custom. According to an ingeniously veiled account in the Talmud, this was the act of a Sadducee, whom the incensed people thereupon pelted almost to death with the Hâdar fruits from the festival boughs (Esrôgim).* This Sadducee was no other than the king himself, and on that

---

* Sukkah 48b.

day he openly espoused the Sadducean cause. And I may say here, in passing, that in this and similar covert statements we cannot fail to recognize a plain intention to do violence to the text of the records—a sort of censorship in ancient days, dictated by a sense either of shame or fear. Of the pelting with the festival fruits Josephus* also speaks, and he adds that the participants paid dearly for it. The Pisidian body-guard made a savage charge on the multitude, of whom six thousand fell on that dreadful day.

This scene of murder and riot had a very important influence on the life of the sorely tried queen. During the long wars which called her husband from home she had probably acted as regent; but now she ceased to take an active part in public affairs, and devoted herself entirely to the education of her young sons. It was not until her brother, Simon ben-Shetach, returned from exile that she came forth from her retirement and again

---

* Antiquities, XIII, 13, 5.

became prominent in political life. Doubtless her return was prompted by the open persecution of the scribes which went hand in hand with the king's espousal of the Sadducean cause. At various times prominent Pharisees were removed from office and banished by the king and his minions; and after the bloody battle of Bethome not less than eight hundred adherents of this persecuted party left their homes and country. Among these fugitives was Simon ben-Shetach. Perhaps, even before this time, the Rabbi had incurred the despot's displeasure by reason of his candor, or, as the authorities state,* he had been slandered by malicious courtiers. Be this as it may, the sage kept himself concealed, but remained in communication with his sister and bided his time. At last the moment came. One day some Persian notabilities appeared at the king's board. "Where is the noble old man," inquired they, " who entertained us so well

---

* Jerushalmi, Berachoth, 7, 2; Nasir, 5, 5; Genesis Rabba, 91.

with his learning in the Law, when we were here last time?" The king was ashamed of his rash deed, gave his consort a hint, and suddenly the president of the Sanhedrin stood before the astonished guests. With calm assurance he seated himself beween the king and queen; and the words with which he justified this rare proceeding have won a place among the world's lofty thoughts. "Thou, O king," said he, "owest this place to thy gold; I, to the Torah."* In this man's nature there was a deplorable incongruity—a strange mingling of elevation of mind with intolerable harshness. As a teacher and systematizer he was without an equal in his age, and his labors fully entitle him to the following high encomium: "The world was desolate; then Simon ben-Shetach arose and restored to the Torah its pristine glory."† But, though nobleminded in all other respects, severity and cruelty were pronounced traits of his char-

---

* Jerushalmi, Berachoth, 7, 2.
† Kiddushin 66a.

acter. The man of whom it is related that he had eighty women executed in one day *—and such statements are never entirely without foundation—has been judged far too leniently by posterity. Nor is it in harmony with Jewish morals that he permitted his own son to be put to death in defence of a principle of law.† For my part, I never had any particular liking for heroes of the stamp of Brutus, and I am glad to say that Brutuses never thrived well on Jewish soil. Nevertheless, with the reappearance of this wise and over-zealous teacher, the Pharisaic party began to prosper again. The Sanhedrin soon freed itself from its Saducean members, and the twenty-eighth of Tebeth, on which this victory was achieved, is inscribed in the old scroll (Megillath Ta'anit) as a day of great rejoicing, which was long observed. So rigidly and implacably did the two great parties confront each other, as to awaken strange

---

* Sanhedrin, 6, 4.

† Jerushalmi, Sanhedrin, 6, 5.

doubts even in the minds of the royal autocrat; and when his weeping spouse implored his last counsel, as he lay on his death-bed, he answered her in these bitter words of irony: "Fear neither the Pharisees nor the party hostile to them. Names count for naught, in all parties there are good and bad men; only be on thy guard against masked hypocrites."*

Long before the Pharisees regained a part of their former prestige, however, Alexander Jannæus had wrested from his enemies some of the pagan cities of Syria and Perea, and forcibly converted them to Judaism."† It is rather singular that the only three conversions to Judaism on a large scale should have been effected by force under Sadducean rule; the Pharisees never cared to spread religion otherwise than with book in hand.

If it is safe to draw a conclusion from the historian's silence on the matter, Salome

---

* Sota 22b.

† Josephus, Antiq., XIII, 15, 4.

Alexandra's two sons must have been excessively fond of her. The royal pair differed widely in their views, tastes, and ambitions; and the sons must have sympathized either with their father or mother. There was certainly some opportunity for the adventurous Aristobulus to assist Jannai in his many military expeditions; for, though younger than his brother, he was old enough to engage actively in war. Yet Josephus, who is always loquacious, has nothing whatever to say on this point. There can be no doubt, therefore, that the two sons felt drawn only to their mother and, finding in her a congenial spirit, must have taken her part. Only on this supposition can we account for the significant omission on the part of the historian.

And now followed a day of tears and mourning. The royal sufferer was left alone again in the cold world, though not quite so forlorn as when Judah Aristobulus died twenty-seven years before. The death of Alexander marks the beginning of the third period of the queen's life, during which she was for nine years a widow and sole ruler. She was now sixty-four, and the stormy vicissitudes of these swiftly following periods had prematurely whitened her hair; yet, surely, among the leaders of her day, none was more worldly-wise, more cautious and discreet than this rare woman.

It was, therefore, a most fortunate occurrence that she, rather than one of her sons, should have succeeded to the throne. Alexander had ample proofs of his wife's abilities and, in spite of his hard nature, was not insensible to her many virtues; was this preference, then, owing to his admiration of her good qualities, or shall we regard it as a result of her own ambition? It is no longer possible to answer this question; but one thing is certain: Israel, in its unsettled political condition, needed to pass through this stage of its development under the peaceful policy of a brave woman, in order to fortify itself better against the inevitable storms of the future.

It is generally admitted that Simon ben-Shetach, in conjunction with Judah ben-Tabai, continued at the head of the Sanhedrin during Alexandra's rule. Satisfactory proof of his having so long retained the office cannot be gathered from the authorities. But, if it be true that the administration of justice was entrusted to so pure and capable a man, the fact sheds new lustre on the royal lady who permitted the great and rigid scribe to have his own way, guaranteeing him the full protection of her high authority in the prosecution of his labors. For it must not be supposed that the highest tribunal of justice was sufficiently protected by its own privileges. History teaches us on every page that justice has much to fear from royalty unless there is a great, liberal-minded sovereign on the throne.

To appreciate the character of Salome Alexandra it is not necessary to dwell minutely on the few events of the last nine years of her reign. Her principal aim was to promote the general prosperity of her country, to dispel the clouds that had gathered during the troublous times of her predecessors; and these results she attained through armed peace, whereby, without stirring the flames of war, her restless neighbors were kept in check. Tradition has painted the blessings of this happy reign in glowing colors. Many years later, pictures of vegetables of uncommon size were exhibited at Jerusalem, such as the peasant's clod yielded in the days of the good queen.*

In her latter years, contemplating with tranquillity the approaching end of her earthly career, she felt some anxiety concerning her son's warlike propensities; and she displayed no little shrewdness in contriving so well to divert him with a sort of mock campaign against Damascus. In the soul of the aged queen there was, indeed, no room for worldly ambition, and it would have been well if the Pharisees had profited by her example. But the baser elements of the party, remembering the wrongs they had suffered under Jannai, took advantage

---

* Taanit 23a.

of the queen's leniency and conducted themselves, in the words of Josephus,* "as if they differed in nothing from lords." The great historian's severe censure of the queen rests solely on these excesses of the Pharisees; for, while doing justice to her rare wisdom and energy, he deplores that "her management during her administration, while she was alive, was such as filled the palace after her death with calamities and disturbance."† In making amends for an injustice so long acquiesced in, and assigning to Salome Alexandra the place among women and sovereigns to which she is justly entitled, the muse of modern history performs one of her noblest tasks.

---

* *Antiq.*, XIII, 16, 2.
† *Ibid.*, XIII, 16, 6.

IV.

MARIAMNE, THE HASMONEAN.

About the year 57 B.C., amid the storms of a turbulent age, Alexander, the adventurous son of Aristobulus II, was united in marriage to his cousin Alexandra, daughter of Hyrcanus. The event occurred shortly after Gabinius the Roman had foiled the ambitious prince in his rash attempt upon the fortresses of Judea. In the children, at least, these nuptials seemed to reconcile fathers who had for a long time been at enmity; but the fates did not smile kindly on the union. Alexandra had been married only nine years, when her young husband was seized by Metellus Scipio, the governor of Syria, carried to Antioch, and there beheaded at the express command of Pompey. He was but twenty-five years of age when he laid his head upon the block. His former acts of rebellion having been pardoned, Alexander's execution, it would seem, was not intended as a punishment for his own misdeeds. It is rather to be ascribed in part to an attempted insurrection of Aristobulus, which had incited the Roman authorities to the severest measures against the unhappy Maccabees, and in part to an inveterate hatred of the entire family.

It was Pompey's habit to invest these political executions with a sort of gloomy Roman splendor, witnessing the butcheries with the ghastly smile of a stoic. Quintus Valerius, an adherent of the popular party and a man of literary attainments, having on one occasion fallen into his power, he walked up and down with his victim for some time, discussing learned matters. At first he was delighted with Valerius' intelligent remarks, but he soon grew tired, summoned the lictors, and bade them despatch him. So we are informed by Plutarch, no mean authority on Roman atrocities.*

The unfortunate Maccabean prince left a widow and two children, Mariamne and

---

* Life of Pompey.

Aristobulus, the third of that name, who were reserved for a bitter fate. Antipater, the crafty Idumean favorite, unmoved by Alexander's ruin, was drawing his snares closer about the doomed family. The office of high-priest continued to be filled for an indefinite term by the weak and confiding Hyrcanus, who was also made nominal ruler; and with so helpless a protector Alexandra and her children had found a sort of refuge.

It was under these circumstances that Herod, the aspiring son of the Idumean counsellor, saw young Mariamne blooming into womanhood with all the inherited beauty of the Maccabees. He ardently desired to possess her, for his calculating shrewdness saw the political advantage of an alliance with the last of the Hasmoneans. His father having been removed by the poisoned cup of his rival Malichus, Herod saw his path clear to the honors and power which he coveted. Fortune favored his designs. Antigonus, the younger brother of the hapless Alexander, having with misguided zeal made an inroad into Judea, the skilful Idumean leader, whose valor and military talents were by far his most conspicuous qualities, found little difficulty in dispersing the undisciplined bands of Antigonus and his confederates. Upon the victor's return to Jerusalem, Hyrcanus foolishly placed the triumphal wreath upon his brow. Excepting only the unfortunate battle of the twenty-third of Sivan in the year 63, when the genius of Judea wept over Pompey's presence and the loss of Jewish independence, this hour, in which a Jewish prince with his own hands crowned his future executioner, is by far the most tragical in its history, now so quickly drawing to a close. Nor did Hyrcanus stop at this exhibition of his favor; in the same eventful year, 42, he gave his consent to Herod's betrothal with the charming Mariamne. Born about the year 56, she was but fourteen when she wedded the man destined to overthrow her family, and who was even then planning the ruin of her uncle Antigonus. Her mother Alexandra looked upon this strange betrothal with conflicting emotions. Witnessing unheard-of deeds in these troubled times, with their shifting interests and almost daily political changes, her heart grew hard and fierce, which readily accounts for her failures and various acts of severity. Herod, then perhaps thirty years of age, upon allying himself with the Hasmonean family, cast off his first wife Doris. This clearly appears from the following passage of Josephus: "So he vented his anger first of all against Antipater's mother, and took away from her all the ornaments which he had given her, which cost a great many talents, and cast her out of the palace a second time."* Can it be that Alexandra's ambition urged him to make such a dangerous concession? The great historian is silent upon the matter, and positively no other reason, conformable with the character of the times and people, can be found.

Meanwhile events took their uninter-

---

* Wars, I, 30, 4.

rupted course. A faint, illusive ray of fortune favored Antigonus' enterprise, and by Alexandra's prudent advice Herod, at the approach of the young commander and his Parthian auxiliaries, fled with his betrothed and his household to the sheltering mountains of Idumea. "Nor could any enemy of his who then saw him in this case be so hard-hearted, but would have commiserated his fortune, while the women drew along their infant children, and left their own country, and their friends in prison, with tears in their eyes, and sad lamentations, and in expectation of nothing but what was of a melancholy nature."*

After some three years, however, there was a complete turn of the tide. The Parthians had been driven out of Syria; Herod, who could obtain anything from Mark Antony by flattery, had received from him the crown of Judea at the Roman capital, the proudest spot of the ancient world; and one of the finest armies that Asia had

---

* Josephus, Antiq., XIV, 13, 7.

ever seen lay encamped before Jerusalem, and was preparing to invest the city closely. In this camp, with the immediate prospect of an inevitable conflict and the slaughter of the besiegers, Herod celebrated his nuptials with Mariamne, to whom he had now been affianced more than four years. This took place in the spring of the year 37, and perhaps it was his love of contrasts, mingling so strangely with his other traits of character, which led him to solemnize the event at such a time.

A few weeks later Mariamne's uncle, the vanquished Antigonus, stood in chains before Herod. Antony would fain have spared him, but the inexorable Herod did not relax his efforts until he had delivered up his harmless rival—harmless now that he had lost his Maccabean courage—to the executioner.* Antigonus was beheaded at Antioch in the summer of the ill-fated year 37; for Graetz's statement† that he died on

---

* Josephus, Antiq., XIV, 16, 4.
† *Geschichte der Juden*, Vol. III, p. 198.

the cross I have not been able to find any warrant. Such were the mournful circumstances attending poor Mariamne's honeymoon.

A brief survey of the political condition of the world at this time is necessary to a proper understanding of the events which follow. For years Antony and Octavius shared the supreme authority, but it was only a question of time when the hollow truce between them would be broken. The political blunders and personal vices of Antony hastened the rupture. His conduct of the Parthian war was marked by all the disaster which springs from indolence and ignorance. What wonder that he no longer cared for affairs of state, when he had thrown himself entirely away upon the fascinating Cleopatra, and while the creatures of this dangerous woman continually surrounded his pavilion and persuaded him to the most pernicious acts! His wicked passion had so completely mastered him, that he shamefully neglected his noble spouse Octavia, the sister of his powerful colleague and one of the most high-minded women of Rome. She followed him to Athens, but he wrote insulting letters to her, forbidding her his presence; and, not content with this, he openly gave away Roman provinces to Cleopatra's sons. The first wrong Octavius bitterly resented. As for the other, while the Roman people could not pardon it, yet with a certain forbearance the Senate declared war not against the guilty Roman statesman, but against the Egyptian queen, and the consequence was that short, decisive campaign known in history as the Battle of Actium.

But in Asia some time elapsed before the true condition of affairs was known, and consequently Cleopatra was in a position to assume a sort of dictatorship over the smaller Roman dependencies; she acted precisely as if the destinies of the empire were already dependent upon her changing whims. Alexandra, putting faith in the Egyptian's pretended favor, was persuaded into adopting a domestic policy which only hastened the ruin both of herself and her family. Nor did Herod, though more prudent, succeed in entirely escaping her influence. Nevertheless, his conduct in this matter represents him at his best. He never acquitted himself so well, he never acted so honorably during his long career. At this time the Idumean was in the full vigor of manhood, before excesses had undermined his health. He was the perfect embodiment of martial dignity and manly beauty, and the siren of the Nile had conceived a violent passion for him. But he vigorously resisted the allurements by which she hoped to entangle him in her snares; he never stained his hands with her blood, though the temptation to rid the world of this pernicious woman was great; and, at the same time, he saved his little kingdom from her all-grasping fangs.* No one that reflects upon these things can deny that the Herod of those days had a claim on the gratitude of Jewish patriots. The relation with

---

* Josephus, Antiq., XV, 4, 2.

Egypt, against which the prophet Jeremiah had long before raised his warning voice, existed but a few days when its first disastrous consequences manifested themselves on the appointment of a successor to the ill-fated Antigonus. The ephod rightfully belonged to some descendant of Aaron; but Herod entirely ignored his brother-in-law Aristobulus, and selected for the office an obscure Babylonian, Ananelus by name. Aristobulus, it is true, was rather young; nevertheless we can easily pardon the maternal pride which led Alexandra to take offence at Herod's conduct. But she did wrong in appealing to Cleopatra, and even to Antony, for assistance in her endeavors to obtain the office for her son. True, she accomplished her immediate purpose. Ananelus was forced to vacate the high-priest's chair, and Aristobulus, who was only seventeen years of age, succeeded him. But, by reason of her secret correspondence with the Egyptian court, Alexandra forfeited the confidence of her son-in-law, who thenceforth kept her a prisoner in the palace.

Chafing under the restraint, she devised a plan by which she and her son, feigning death, were to be carried in coffins to the banks of the Nile; but the plot being discovered, the fate of the young Maccabean was sealed. Perhaps the Idumean would have acted less quickly, had not the ill-considered display of sympathy for Aristobulus, on the part of the people, fanned his smothered fury into a flame. For when the priest, now eighteen, stood at the altar on the Feast of Tabernacles, in all the beauty of blooming youth, a murmur of applause ran through the great crowds gathered on the hill of the Temple, inasmuch as, by the usurpation of the slave's son, עֶבֶד בִּישָׁא, as Herod was called in suppressed rage,* the Hasmonean family had grown not a little in popular favor.

A few days after this occurrence, several youths were bathing in a pond at Jericho. While engaged in this apparently harmless sport, one of the number was forced under

---

* Baba bat. 4a.

water by his companions and kept there until life was extinct. When the body was taken out, it was found to be that of no less a person than Aristobulus, the high-priest; the others were assassins hired by Herod. This happened in the year 35 B.C. Poor Mariamne! To how dangerous a man had she allied herself! Alexander, Antigonus, and young Aristobulus—three illustrious victims from this ill-starred house in so short a time!

For this atrocious deed Herod was now summoned to appear before the Roman ruler at Laodicea. But why? we naturally ask. One murder more or less made very little difference to the Roman authorities. And, besides, was not this purely a matter of local concern? Our text-books and annalists have shed no light on the subject; even Graetz views it only in its external bearings. Josephus, it is true, furnishes us with all the historical facts, but he is too little of a pragmatic historian to draw the proper inference from his own premises. Without recourse to the pragmatic method, however, we can obtain no satisfactory answer to our question. Beyond all doubt Mark Antony had the best of reasons for thus taking Herod to task; for, in the absence of some such supposition, the stony-hearted Idumean's dread remains wholly inexplicable. These reasons are not very far to seek. There was a turn in the tide of Mark Antony's fortunes. As we well know, rulers never guard their rights and privileges so jealously as when their power is on the decline, and the triumvir's brilliant career was rapidly nearing its end. Of this the crafty Herod was well aware; he had already determined on a plan of approaching Octavius when the proper time arrived; but his well-laid schemes were now to be frustrated by Antony's unseasonable anger. And now we can easily understand the cause of Herod's apprehensions. Besides, we must not forget another circumstance. The sensual Roman, who had seen a picture of Aristobulus,* had for some time

---

* Josephus, Antiq., XIV, 2, 6 and 7.

taken a personal interest in the handsome youth.

Herod accordingly repaired to Laodicea to conduct his defence. Upon the disastrous consequences of this journey we shall touch but lightly, it being no part of our purpose to write a biography of the wicked king. Before his departure, he committed the government to his confidant Joseph, an uncle of his and also the first husband of his sister Salome, and secretly instructed him to put Mariamne to death, if he should be deprived of his own life by Antony. In his passionate love for his beautiful wife he now displayed, for the first time, all the cruel, brutish instincts of the Idumean nature—a savage ferocity which Jewish culture had not been able to subdue. He loved her, and would therefore surrender her to no successor, least of all to Antony. Is there not something in this man's character that reminds us of England's crowned Blue-beard, Henry VIII? Bad as it is to be hated by others, it is infinitely better than to be loved by such monsters. They kiss and embrace their favorites, it is true; but their very caresses are torture.

Through Joseph's indiscretion Mariamne learned the fate that awaited her in the event of Herod's death. The hapless woman had once loved the tyrant, and, pardoning his cruel jealousy, she loved him again with all the intensity of which her pure soul was capable. During eleven years of wedded life she bore him five children, of whom one son and two daughters died in infancy. The two surviving sons, Alexander and Aristobulus, were reserved for a mournful death—a death that covered their unnatural father with fresh ignominy. As matters now stood, Mariamne could do nothing in her sorrow except loathe her husband, and, alas! there was to be no lack of fuel for the hatred which took possession of her. The secret which Joseph had betrayed cost him his life, the fatal blow being dealt without a trial or sentence. Mariamne herself was his accuser. Openhearted and sincere, she upbraided her spouse with his cruel conduct, and, though he only smiled incredulously when the same thing had previously been reported to him by his mother Cypros and his sister Salome, the two evil demons of his house, the despot did not hesitate a moment to believe *her*. And now Nemesis began speedily to do her work in the Idumean's family; with each twig of the Hasmonean trunk that fell beneath the blow of the tyrant's axe, he was incited to acts of equal violence against his own flesh and blood, as witness the cruel fates of Joseph, Castoboras, Pheroras and Antipater.

Meanwhile more than four years passed away, but no comfort came to the afflicted Mariamne. She was still young, still at an age when women, even though they be not queens, have aspirations which they expect to realize, and, in spite of her tribulations, her beauty was unchanged. Herod's palace had grown to be a veritable pandemonium, the limbo of Dante's Hell could not have furnished a more melancholy sight. Herod had from time to time added four or more women to his harem, so that polygamy, which seemed to have been practically abolished by the example of the Hebrew kings, prophets, rabbis, and other eminent men, was now revived by him in its most repulsive form. The consequences can easily be imagined. Eight or more passionate women, hating each other with all the hate of deadly enemies, were constantly thrown together in the halls and galleries of the palace; courtiers, eunuchs, hirelings, barbers, sycophants, maids, moved to and fro in large numbers, regaling this or that mistress with their idle gossip.

And regard for the truth compels us to censure her, too, whom we would fain spare on account of her misfortunes. Mariamne was by no means the gentlest in this chaotic household. With various other traits of the Hasmonean character, she especially inherited their inflexible pride, bluntness, and harsh arrogance. Even Josephus, though obviously partial to her, admits that "she treated her husband imperiously enough, because she saw he was so fond of her as to be enslaved to her. She did not also consider seasonably with herself that she lived under a monarchy, and that she was at another's disposal, and accordingly would behave herself after a saucy manner to him, which yet he usually put off in a jesting way, and bore with moderation and good temper. She would also expose his mother and his sister openly, on account of the meanness of their birth, and would speak unkindly of them."*

Meanwhile, on September 2, B.C. 31, the naval battle of Actium had been fought, which in a trice changed the political complexion of the world. The Jewish vassal prepared to journey to Rhodes, in order to cajole his new liege lord into pardoning his faithful allegiance to Antony for so many years. But, before leaving, Herod took care to rid himself of all the dangerous elements in the Maccabean party; for, in case his plans failed, even the weakest representative of that race might have served as a rallying-point for malcontents. Accord-

---

* Antiq., XV, 7, 4.

ingly, the aged Hyrcanus, now in his seventy-fifth year,* to whom Herod owed all his good fortune, had to suffer death. He was very quickly executed in the palace. The particulars are omitted as unessential. Weakness is sometimes so near akin to wickedness and even to crime, that his doom, I venture to assert, was not altogether undeserved. Josephus never tires of lauding his gentle disposition; but he says nothing in condemnation of Hyrcanus' moral cowardice, which cost many of the ablest men their lives and put an end to the liberty of Judea. Judaism regards life too seriously to excuse the vacillations of a *roi débonnaire;* such a nonentity does not in any age deserve to be leniently dealt with by the historian. Moreover, only a few persons mourned the loss of the aged man, and his granddaughter Mariamne was certainly not among

---

* Josephus (Antiq., XV, 6, 3) makes him above eighty years old; but this is most unlikely, for he could hardly have been born before the year 105. Josephus is not always to be relied upon for dates, owing to his predilection for round numbers.

them; for it was the death of her father
and her brother, not the execution of her
grandfather, with which, in a fatal hour,
she reproached her husband.* She had not
yet forgotten, we may be sure, that it was
the thoughtless Hyrcanus who cast her in
the Idumean's arms.

Nevertheless, the destruction of her world-
weary grandsire was a sure precursor of the
dreadful fate reserved for the brilliant
Hasmonean herself. Herod was now about
to start on his journey, the preparations
attending his departure for Laodicea being
for the most part repeated with much
greater caution and severity. The females
of his household were placed in safe custody.
Not content this time, however, with simply
confining Mariamne in the palace, he sent
her and her mother to the fortress Alexan-
drium, and put them in charge of his
treasurer Joseph and of Sohemus the
Iturean. These men received the same
secret order, which, four years before, had

---

* Antiq., XV, 7, 4.

cost another Joseph—Herod's uncle—his life. If he should fail in his undertaking, the two women were to be executed by their custodians.

On account of the striking similarity of the circumstances, there really was no secret to keep; the imprisoned women must have been stupid indeed not to anticipate a repetition of Herod's cruel injunction. Yet our historian has a great deal to say about Sohemus' indiscreet talk, and represents him as having suffered death for the same offence for which Herod's uncle, Joseph, was executed. It is just possible, however, that Sohemus may have been put out of the way for quite a different reason, since every petty scheme of Herod's to advance the interests of his house involved the inevitable slaughter of one or more innocent persons. It was part and parcel of the policy of the court.

I am, therefore, inclined to think that Mariamne's doom was sealed before Herod set out on his journey of homage. The aversion with which she recoiled from him when he returned, puffed up with the favor Augustus had shown him; the open disgust with which his caresses filled her,—this rapid change of affection to hate served but to hasten the inevitable end. How were it possible for a noble woman to live any longer with such a man! She had but one haven of rest—death, and death alone.

And amid such conditions began the year 29 B.C. Hate, injured pride, and jealousy had for the moment so far overcome the love which Mariamne's fascinating charms still kept aglow in the despot's breast, that, maddened with rage, he consented to have her condemned to death by a venal court. A good pretext for seeking her destruction was soon found. There was no occasion for Salome to invent the story that Mariamne had prepared a poisoned draught or love potion for the king. As if the unfortunate woman had not already suffered enough, another bitter drop was added to her overflowing cup from a source whence she had least expected it. Alexandra, her unnatural mother, in order to purchase the tyrant's good-will, cast off her daughter and pursued her with such vile abuse, while the uncomplaining sufferer was led to the place of execution, that it excited the indignation of the spectators. But the queen's last moments cannot be better portrayed than in the matchless words of Josephus: "At the first she gave her not a word, nor was discomposed at her peevishness, and only looked at her, yet did she, out of a greatness of soul, discover her concern for her mother's offence, and especially for her exposing herself in a manner so unbecoming her: but as for herself, she went to her death with an unshaken firmness of mind, and without changing the color of her face, and thereby evidently discovered the nobility of her descent to the spectators, even in the last moments of her life."*

For having thus softened the painful details of this death-scene with an artist's skilful touch, we owe Flavius Josephus a debt of gratitude. As the Greeks in Euripides' masterpiece, *Hecuba*, cover the body of the

---

* Antiq., XV, 7, 5.

dying Polyxena with ivy leaves to hide it from view, so the famous annalist magnanimously throws the veil of his lofty compassion over the bleeding remains of this true queen. Had Josephus written nothing else of worth, this one paragraph alone entitles him to a place among the greatest writers.

We have heard so much of Mariamne's moral purity and nobility of soul, that we are naturally led to ask whether she did not possess the virtues of the better Maccabees. It cannot be denied that we miss in her the Hasmonean piety, the devotion of the Chasidim, their humility and unselfish patriotism. And to the absence of these virtues must be ascribed the mysterious fact that precisely where we should expect to find an account of the tragedy of her life—in rabbinical literature, that workshop of Judaism, —no mention whatever is made of it. Had her nature taken on more of the polish of Jewish life, who knows but that she might have been reserved for a better fate or died in a better cause! Who knows but that history might to-day have placed her at the side of her great ancestress, the honored Salome Alexandra! But the later Hasmoneans were bent on furthering their own worldly interests, apart from the higher aspirations of their people; and the nation, through its best minds, duly avenged itself by ignoring them as unpatriotic and selfishly ambitious.

Mariamne was but twenty-seven years of age, when her cruel husband condemned her to death. Of her position in the world's literature I cannot speak, as I have read none of the various tragedies and other productions of which she forms the central figure.

During more than twenty-six years she lived on in her murderer's memory, to torture his soul with remorse; and this circumstance inspired the following well-known stanzas, from the Hebrew Melodies, where Byron gives a most vivid picture of the grief-stricken despot lamenting her for whose untimely death he had only himself to blame.

"Oh, Mariamne! Now for thee
　The heart for which thou bledst is bleeding;
Revenge is lost in agony,
　And wild remorse to rage succeeding.
Oh, Mariamne! Where art thou?
　Thou canst not hear my bitter pleading:
Ah! couldst thou—thou wouldst pardon now,
　Though Heaven were to my prayer unheeding.

"And is she dead? And did they dare
　Obey my frenzy's jealous raving?
My wrath but doomed my own despair:
　The sword that smote her 's o'er me waving.
But thou art cold, my murdered love!
　And this dark heart is vainly craving
For her who soars alone above,
　And leaves my soul unworthy saving.

"She's gone, who shared my diadem;
　She sunk, with her my joys entombing;
I swept that flower from Judah's stem
　Whose leaves for me alone were blooming;
And mine's the guilt, and mine the hell,
　This bosom's desolation dooming;
And I have earned those tortures well,
　Which unconsumed are still consuming!"

Alexandra did not long enjoy the fruits of her unnatural conduct and base hypocrisy. The sword that had ended the beautiful Mariamne's life was already whetted to cut off the head of her guiltier mother, and after the expiration of only a few weeks she fell a victim to her reckless and incessant political machinations.

V.

HELENA, QUEEN AND PROSELYTE.

To the east of the river Tigris, between its tributaries Lycus and Caprus (now called the great and little Zab), there lies a small but fertile stretch of country which, under the name of Adiabene, once formed an important dependency of the Parthian empire. About the time of which we are now speaking this province was under the rule of an ancient race of princes, some of whom were specially distinguished for their excellent qualities. The country itself is exceedingly small in extent—the whole area being comprised within 35° 30′ and 36° 30′ north latitude; and, up to the first century of our era, its sole claim to fame rested on the victory of Alexander the Great near the old capital Arbela (now Arbil), which was achieved in 331 B.C. But, about the period of its history with which we are here concerned, the Adiabenian annals are adorned with the names of a far greater number of high-minded sovereigns than we should then have expected to find at the Asiatic courts. In the present sketch we shall speak in particular of an august royal lady, whose life is most deserving of the reader's attention.

Helena—the הילני המלכה of the Talmud*—was born probably about the year 15 B.C. In conformity with the depraved custom of Oriental dynasties, a custom for which, as Graetz† correctly observes, the Macedonian court was chiefly to blame, she was married to a near relative; according to Josephus,‡ her own brother. By her marriage with king Monobazus I she had two sons, of whom the younger, Izates, born in the year 5 C.E., became his father's idol. The details of the king's partiality for Izates are of too little importance to be recounted in so brief a historical sketch; suffice it to say, that he

---

* Nasir, 3, 6 ; Tosefta, Sukkah, 1, *et al.*

† *Geschichte der Juden*, III, 332.

‡ Antiq., XX, 2, 1.

preferred him not only to his elder brother, afterwards Monobazus II, but also to the sons of his other wives. In order, however, to protect Izates from the envious hatred of his brothers, the boy's education was entrusted to king Abennerig, a friend of his father, who reigned over Charax-Spasinu, on the northern coast of the Persian Gulf. In his new home young Izates found not only a second father, but also a wife in the person of the king's daughter, Samacha; he gained something else, moreover, which proved to be of great value to him in after life.

While Izates was residing here, a Jewish merchant, Ananias by name, paid frequent visits to Abennerig's court. He was a man well versed in the Scriptures, and, in offering his dainty and rare wares to the ladies of the palace, it was but natural for him to talk about the Bible now and then, and to teach them "to worship God according to the Jewish religion."* What has often

---

* Josephus, Antiq., XX, 2, 3.

been observed in thousands of cases, before and afterwards, at Rome, Damascus, and other places, happened in this instance. Noble women grew enthusiastic in their praise of the spiritual beauty of Judaism, and particularly were they impressed with the difference between the position of Jewish women and that of their heathen sisters; the former treated with respect, the latter held in degrading subjection. It was among the ladies of the palace that Izates first came in contact with the eloquent Jewish missionary, by whom he was so greatly influenced that he became an ardent convert; probably, too, his wife Samacha had set him the example by adopting the Jewish faith herself.

His favorite son having now been absent many years, the elder Monobazus, who had grown quite old, naturally longed to see him once more; and when, at his father's command, Izates prepared to return to Adiabene, so earnest was he in his zeal for his new confession that he persuaded Ananias to accompany him. The king of Adiabene did not long survive this meeting with his son; he died shortly after, in the year 35 C.E. But before his father's death, Izates made the surprising discovery that his mother had become a Jewess. During her son's absence Helena had made the acquaintance of a Jewish teacher of the Law, and through his instruction she was led to abjure paganism; whether or not this was done with her husband's sanction, we are not informed.

The death of Monobazus I marks the greatest epoch in the history of the Adiabenian dynasty; for, after the old king had passed away, Judaism at once became a power in the affairs of the state, its civilizing influence being plainly visible in all subsequent events. The first matter of importance was to settle the succession to the throne. Izates had been singled out for the crown by his father's capricious favor; but this testamentary provision, if any of those interested refused to give their assent, could be carried into effect only by a bloody revolution in the palace, and such a scene of horror the pious queen wished to prevent. She accordingly convoked the grandees of the realm, communicated to them the late king's wish, and asked their counsel. The nobles were content to acknowledge Izates as king; but they suggested the necessity of putting all the other princes to death, after the true Oriental fashion, in order to render his position secure. The noble-minded Helena was shocked at this terrible proposal, and it required all her tact to prevent an atrocity sanctioned by the custom of the age.

On account of Izates' absence from court —he had gone to the province conferred on him by his father—Monobazus, the elder brother, acted as regent; only for a few days, however, for Izates presently arrived at the capital. Then Monobazus, with the consent of all concerned, voluntarily surrendered the reins of government to his younger brother. The new king immediately released his brothers and relatives, who, according to the prevailing practice, had all been imprisoned. But in order, at the same time, to guard his throne against revolts and ambitious schemes, he hit upon the expedient of banishing the princes: one-half he sent to the imperial palace at Rome, where they were still living during the emperor Claudius' reign;* the other half, to the Parthian king Artabanus III at Ctesiphon.

With his elevation to the throne, Izates lost none of his enthusiasm for Judaism. All his religious duties were performed with the utmost conscientiousness. He could not rest satisfied with the assurance of his teacher Ananias that the observance of the Abrahamic covenant was not incumbent upon a גר תושב, a proselyte of the gate; he preferred to follow the more orthodox view of one Eleazer of Galilee, who held this ceremony to be binding on all proselytes alike.† As bearing upon a theological dispute which has arisen in more recent days, this historical incident is of more than passing interest.

---

*Josephus, Antiq., XX, 2, 3.
† *Ibid.*, XX, 4.

The first few years of the royal proselyte's reign were blessed with undisturbed peace and general prosperity. When his suzerain, Artabanus, was driven from his throne and kingdom for the second time, about 41 C.E., Izates loyally espoused the fallen monarch's cause, mediated between him and his discontented subjects, and compelled the usurper Kinnamus to abdicate.* The reinstated king showed his gratitude by adding the district of Nisibis to Adiabene.

But this condition of things did not last long. Artabanus dying in 42 C.E., the Parthian empire again became the scene of long-protracted disturbances, into which, much to his sorrow, Izates was also drawn. Bardanes, Artabanus' successor, wished to force his feudatory to take part in the war against Rome, and was just about to chastise him for his refusal when he himself was slain by conspirators.† So, at least, we are told in the account which Josephus

---

* Rawlinson, *The Sixth Oriental Monarchy*, VI, 14.

† Tacitus, Annals, XI, 10.

gives of this affair. Tacitus, however, makes express mention of Izates' encounter with all-powerful Rome;* but the combat is stated to have taken place sometime after the year 46 C.E., which could not have been prior to the reign of the Parthian Gotarzes. The Talmud here appears to side with the Roman historian, for the war spoken of in Nazir., III, 6, which also delayed Helena's intended pilgrimage to Jerusalem, seems, in view of the surrounding circumstances, to refer, unmistakably, not to the later military exploits of Izates, but to the struggle with Rome.† Besides, if Dio Cassius may be trusted,‡ the Roman war must have dragged along for many more years than is commonly supposed, nay, it must have outlasted Izates' reign, inasmuch as peace was concluded by his successor Monobazus II, who gave hostages to the Romans

Through his brother's conversion, Mono-

---

* Annals, XII, 13, 14.

† *Cf.* also Hamburger, *Real-Encyclopædie*, II, 802.

‡ lxii, 23.

bazus and other members of the royal house were led to embrace the Jewish faith. The courage and publicity with which they did so roused the anger of the pagan Adiabenians, and accordingly they rose up in revolt against their ruler. But Izates, who had been unfortunate for a while, again prospered in his undertakings, nor did fortune ever again entirely desert him. The Arabian king, Abia, to whom the rebellious magnates had appealed for assistance, suffered so disastrous a defeat, that in despair he put an end to his life. Vologases, who occupied the Parthian throne at Ctesiphon since 52 C.E., thereupon took the field in person against his feudatory. He was at the head of a strong army, but, on learning that robber hordes had broken into his own provinces, he was obliged to turn back without having accomplished anything.

I have thus outlined Izates' political career, for a period almost co-extensive with his reign, in order not only to present the historical events in their unbroken sequence, but also for the purpose of showing how clearly the good influence of Helena's faithful observance of the Jewish moral laws manifests itself in both the court policy and the general conduct of her sons. In what follows, however, I shall confine myself more particularly to the life of the widowed queen. As soon as Izates ceased for a time to be so busily occupied with affairs of state, she made use of her sad leisure to carry out a long-cherished project. Having heard a great deal of Jerusalem, and her reverence for Judaism increasing daily, she was seized with a longing to visit the incomparable Temple, the only place of worship of the kind in the world. The anxious mother had made a vow to lead the life of a Nazarite for seven years, in the event of her son's safe return from the war, by which, as already indicated, the Roman campaign is meant. When, at last,—about the year 45 C.E.—a brief interval of peace succeeded, Izates not only gave his consent to his mother's journey, but also aided her royally in her preparations.

As Adiabene is at some distance from Palestine, the news of the pious queen's project could not but have excited great interest and curiosity long in advance of her arrival; and when, after many days of suspense, the foreign train with its numerous attendants made its entrance through one of the north-eastern gates, the Fish-gate perhaps, it is certain that the Holy City was alive with joyous excitement. Would that I had the brilliant, glowing colors of Byzantine art, or the resources of an Alma Tadema or Benjamin Constant, the modern imitators of that school, that I might depict this reception in all its gorgeous magnificence! The flowing robes, the rustling brocades, the peculiar features of the long line of attendants, captivating the eye by their strangeness, the central figure of the queen in her royal palanquin amid the surging crowd, who gazed on eagerly in the proud consciousness of the honor conferred on their city—all this pomp, glitter, and commotion beneath the glorious splendor of the Eastern sun, how grand a spectacle it must have been! Helena's arrival dispelled for a moment the deep gloom of tyranny and oppression which was settling upon hapless Judea. After the murder of good king Agrippa, Rome had sent another of her pliant tools, the procurator Cuspius Fadus, to Jerusalem. He it was who now ruled over Judea; and the bitter envy, the spiteful derision, with which the Roman officials must have witnessed this moral victory of the down-trodden Palestineans, can be better imagined than described.

But Helena had not come to parade foreign splendor. She was now sixty-four, and led a very retired life, devoting herself almost exclusively to pious works. From the disciples of Hillel she ascertained the conditions of nazariteship required by the Law, and, some unimportant incident having delayed the execution of her design, she lived under the self-imposed restrictions of a Nazarite for fourteen long years—almost the remainder of her life.* She divided her time between Jerusalem and Lydda, and in Acra, one of the quarters of

---

* Nazir, III, 6; Gemara, *ibid.*, 20a.

the former city, she erected a magnificent palace, which fell a prey to the flames of the destructive year 70.* This was not the only splendid edifice with which the Adiabenian line beautified the capital. Somewhat later perhaps, Helena's younger relative, Grapte, erected an equally extensive building in the quarter known as Ophel.† Even at this time influential scholars were living at Lydda, who were fond of resorting to the house of the high-minded queen. While in this provincial town, during the Feast of Tabernacles,—so the Tosefta‡ tells us—she was on one occasion sitting in her bower, which in her *naïveté* she had built in the huge proportions prompted by her Eastern love of display, when her rabbinical friends entered. The politic sophrim, noticing at once this violation of the Halachic ordinance,§ very pardonable in a prose-

---

* Josephus, Wars, VI, 6, 3.
† *Ibid.*, IV, 9, 11.
‡ Sukkah, I.
§ A sukkah must not exceed twenty cubits in height. (Sukkah, I, 1.)

lyte, only smiled inwardly, without uttering so much as a word of comment.

When Helena went to Jerusalem, she was accompanied by the five sons of Izates, who received there an education in keeping with the religious spirit of the place.* Her two sons, Izates and Monobazus, often stopped at the Judean capital, and other Adiabenians of rank from time to time followed the example of their generous princes. For more than a century from this date, as can be demonstrated, the Jewish race and the inhabitants of the small Parthian fief were on terms of the most friendly intercourse.† It is very necessary, however, for Jewish writers to make a thorough investigation of such epochal conversions, and especially of those on a large scale, with a view to determine their genuineness. This is indispensable, if for no better reason than because the most important events of this kind, *e.g.*, the Khazar conversion of the eighth cen-

---

* Josephus, Antiquities, XX, 3, 4.

† Hamburger, *Real-Encyclopædie*, II, 18.

G

tury, are either designedly ignored or else denied by many Christian scholars of the present day.

The Adiabenian dynasty soon won renown in Jerusalem and throughout the rest of Palestine by their great acts of benevolence. Long after Helena's arrival at Jerusalem, about 47 C.E., a dire famine prevailed in Judea, which must have continued for years, as Josephus speaks of it twice in connection with the maladministration of two procurators, Cuspius Fadus and Tiberius Alexander.* The generous queen had corn bought up in Alexandria, and figs in Cyprus, at an enormous outlay, and distributed these provisions in bulk among the famishing people. When her son heard of the calamity, eager not to be outdone by his good mother, he sent very large sums of money to the principal men of Jerusalem for the same charitable purpose; and at this very time—what a contrast!—a degenerate scion of Israel was ruling over Jerusalem by means of the

---

* Antiq., XX, 2, 5 and 5, 2.

sword, cross, and scourge, in the name of rapacious Rome. Tiberius Alexander, the son of a noble father, Alexander Lysimachus, alabarch of Alexandria, and of a still nobler uncle, the philosopher Philo, had not only, through some unaccountable perversion of the best influences of home, turned recreant to the grand traditions of his ancestors; he had not only renounced the God of Israel for Jupiter Capitolinus and all the other superstitions of Roman mythology; but he was, moreover, one of the most abandoned apostates that disgrace the history of the Jewish race. Josephus, to whom the details of this man's life were quite familiar, has, much to his own discredit, purposely concealed three-fourths of his misdeeds. Even in the two or three crimes of which he accuses the wicked procurator, the great historian plainly palters with the truth, being doubtless actuated by the desire not to give offence to his Roman friends. A careful reading of the paragraph to which I refer*

---

* Antiq., XX, 5, 2.

will convince the reader of the justice of my charge. Here we find another instance of that censorship, practised in antiquity and dictated by the fear of men and princes, to which I was the first to call attention. While now this apostate hireling of mighty Rome found glory, nay, savage delight, in whetting the Roman sword for the necks of his own brethren, there sat in her palace at Acra an august lady, who had journeyed thither from the distant table-land of Assyria, and who, though belonging to quite a different race, was so closely allied to the Jewish people in her thoughts and feelings, that she sympathized with them in all their woes, and spent almost a life-time in trying to heal some of the many wounds which this degenerate man had inflicted on his land and people.

In the account given by Josephus of Helena's visit to Jerusalem, after relating the matters on which we have touched, he promises to speak later of her other acts of munificence;* but, as sometimes hap-

---

* Antiq., XX, 2, 5.

pens with busy writers, he fails to redeem his promise. Perhaps he referred to Helena's valuable gifts to the Temple, of which special mention is made in the Talmud. She dedicated a golden candlestick to the sanctuary,* or, as the Gemara† defines it, a concave mirror, whose reflected rays, indicating the hour of sunrise, served to mark the proper time for reciting the Shema; and also a golden tablet, on which the section Sota (concerning the suspected wife, Numbers, V, 11-31) was engraved. The example of his mother excited in Monobazus a spirit of generous rivalry, and accordingly he provided with golden handles ‡ all the sacred vessels used on the Day of Atonement. Of the life of this man history has left us very scanty records, evidently because his reign extended beyond the period to which Josephus proposed to confine himself; but ancient

---

* Joma III, 10.

† 37b.

‡ Tosefta, Joma II.

traditions single him out as by far the most charitable of his race. His liberality became a positive passion; and when, on one occasion, his relatives reproached him with having, in a year of scarcity, distributed among the poor almost all the treasures inherited from his ancestors, the magnanimous Adiabenian replied in the following lofty words, which have been handed down to posterity: "My fathers garnered riches for this world, I garner for brighter realms; they deposited their wealth where human hands may seize it, I have placed mine beyond human reach; they amassed treasures that yield nothing, those gathered by me produce a large revenue; they accumulated money and money's worth, I gain men's gratitude; they hoarded for others, I hoard for myself; my ancestors, in fine, gathered for this life alone, I lay up store in the other world for all time to come."* What greater glory could Helena have asked, even if this were all she

---

* Tosefta, Pea IV.

had done, than that of having brought up such sons?

Izates' well-spent life drew to a close in the year 60 C.E; he died at the age of fifty-five, after a reign of nearly a quarter of a century. When the royal mother heard of her dear son's decease, his memory impelled her irresistibly to return to her native land. Though now in her seventy-fifth year, she suffered no great inconvenience from the journey; it was vouchsafed her to reach the spot where her favorite son had expired with her name upon his dying lips, and here she lingered to bedew the dead body with her tears. Only a few days later, she, too, passed away. Monobazus, succeeding Izates upon the throne, had the revered remains of his mother and brother carried to Jerusalem, and placed in the mausoleum destined for them. Hard by the northern wall of the Holy City, which divided the suburb Bezetha from the open country, and only one-third of a mile distant from the lower town (Acra), stood a huge marble pile, built in the Græco-Egyptian style.

Helena had had this showy structure erected in her life-time, as a final resting-place for the bodies of herself and family. This is the same tomb which Pausanias saw at a later date, and must not be confounded with the well-known sepulchres of the kings; it lies somewhat farther to the west, very near the tower of Psephinus.

The Jewish race gratefully cherished the memory of good queen Helena far down into the Middle Ages. In a later Midrash* she occupies a conspicuous place among ten royal proselytes. Nor must it be forgotten that this noble-hearted dynasty continued true to the Jewish nation to the very last. On the day when Cestius Gallus, attacking Jerusalem, was forced by Jewish valor to make a most ignominious retreat, two kinsmen of the royal house, Monobazus and Kenedeus, perished on the field of honor,† and they were not the only Adiabenians who unsheathed their swords in

---

* Beth-Hamidrash, ed. Jellinek, IV, p. 133, *et seq.*

† Josephus, Wars, II, 19, 2.

the deadly struggle for Jewish independence. When the tragic end came, the remaining members of this high-minded family naturally incurred the wrath of Titus, though, by his determination to take them with him to Rome as hostages, they escaped a much worse fate.*

---

* Josephus, Wars, VI, 6, 4.

VI.

BERENICE.

The daughter of Agrippa I, called Berenice—a favorite name among the Alexandrian Greeks—was born in the year 28 C.E. If we except a certain kindness of heart, such as persons of lax morals and loose habits often possess, this woman's life presents very little worthy of commendation. I hardly feel at liberty, however, to omit all mention of her, not only because her career is intimately bound up with the history of that turbulent century, but also because her very shortcomings serve admirably to characterize the kind of women— not a very exalted or attractive class, to be sure—that we might naturally expect to find amid the vicissitudes of the Herodian house, nay, that we must of necessity find under such mental and moral conditions, with their manifold allurements and temptations.

Berenice's personal charms brought her numerous suitors, while she was yet very young. Historians speak of her striking beauty, which disturbed for a moment the tranquillity of mighty Rome itself, in terms of extravagant praise. She was probably still a child, when her father married her to Marcus, son of Alexander Lysimachus, the rich and highly educated alabarch of Alexandria. But Marcus died very soon after he was united to his charming wife, and thus the young princess was left a widow even in her childhood. Knowing from his own adventurous youth that it was not well for his daughter to remain single, the king lost no time in giving her again in marriage. She now became the spouse of her uncle Herod, to whom, through the intercession of his brother and father-in-law, the emperor Claudius granted the Syrian principality of Chalcis. Shortly after, in the year 44, her father died, most likely through poison, and about the same time Berenice, then not above sixteen, appears to have lost her second husband. She was now placed under the guardianship of her brother, Agrippa II, concerning whose relations to his sister malicious tongues whispered a most damaging story. Doubtless these rumors were not without foundation, as Josephus* reluctantly admits; and certainly could it have been consistently done, Titus' subsequent *liaison* with Berenice would have induced him, for the Roman's sake, to pass over the matter in silence. But, as Juvenal's celebrated satire† fully attests, the affair had already been noised abroad through the medium of Roman literature. In the hope of putting an end to the evil reports concerning her, Berenice, after many years of widowhood, not very creditably spent, entered into the nuptial state for the third time. A petty Asiatic king, Polemo of Cilicia, influenced by Berenice's charms and bribed by Herod's gold, embraced the Jewish faith for the purpose of marrying her. Soon growing tired of Polemo, how-

---

* Antiq., XX, 7, 3.

† VI, 157, *et seq.*

ever, she deserted him in order that she might be perfectly free to follow her own unrestrained inclinations, while he, on his part, returned to his former faith. Her two sisters, Mariamne and Drusilla, deserve to be censured almost as severely as she for their dissolute lives; in imitation of Roman depravity, they were continually changing husbands—a custom which very soon found its way to the East, where it was made attractive under new forms. Of her youngest sister, the beautiful, blooming Drusilla, Berenice was very envious and subjected her to all manner of annoyances.

The character of these women shows us how low the Herodians had sunk in Berenice's time. The seed sown by bloodthirsty Herod had borne poisonous fruit, and in these scions of the Idumean stock, forcibly engrafted on Judaism, scarcely a vestige of Israel's spiritual nature can be discerned. But, however little Jewish history need concern itself with the wanton misdeeds of the Herodians, particularly on the female side,—misdeeds causing them not alone to drift away entirely from Judaism, but also hastening that proud family's doom—it is provoking to find that among the Romans, as may be observed in the contemptuous tone of their writers, these outcasts should have been regarded as true representatives of the Jewish race. There is but one way to account for this error: the victorious Romans were so inflated with conceit, that they rarely troubled themselves to inquire minutely into matters which concerned only their subjects.

Meanwhile the awful catastrophe that befell Judea was vigorously approaching. The last and worst of the procurators, Gessius Florus, came to Jerusalem with the determination to stir up the angry passions of the inhabitants by new acts of violence, in order that he might find in their measures of self-defence some sort of pretext to rob and murder them. In the month of May, 66 C.E., his brutal cohorts burst into the Upper Market Place, to begin their work of pillage and slaughter. Berenice chanced to be in the capital at the time; a nazaritic vow, it is said, made her presence there a necessity.* How strange a contrast even in these strangely turbulent times—this frivolous descendant of Herod in the role of an abstinent, pious Nazarite! The sight of the horrible scenes enacted before her very eyes awakened the better impulses of her nature; the Maccabean blood in her veins boiled at these excesses of Roman insolence; the sacred character of her surroundings excited within her a feeling of pity for the people who, in spite of the lustre which they had shed on her house, were now being goaded on to destruction by her own family. She sent her servants and the officers of her household before the tribunal of the cruel Florus, to intercede for the unhappy Jews; nay, she herself stood barefoot before the tyrant, conjuring, imploring him to put a stop to the atrocities—but all in vain. Obliged to conceal herself in her palace, Berenice remained during the entire night exposed to the utmost danger, having

---

* Josephus, Wars, II, 15, 1.

no other protection against the fury of the Roman soldiery than that which the guards of her household afforded her. This event occurred on the 16th of Ijar (the Artemisius of Macedonian chronology) of the troublous year 66.

Some days later her brother Agrippa returned home. He had been at Alexandria, where he congratulated the apostate Tiberius Alexander, the alabarch's degenerate son, on his good fortune in having secured the office of governor of Egypt. The alabarch was closely related to the Herodian house by various intermarriages: his elder son, Marcus, had been Berenice's first husband, and the other son, Demetrius, had wedded Mariamne, Berenice's younger sister. The news of the outrages committed in Jerusalem had no doubt hastened Agrippa's return; he flattered himself that he could persuade the national party to submit to Rome, hoping thereby to increase his influence with the Roman authorities. For this purpose he delivered his celebrated oration in favor of peace, which has been transmitted to us too fully by Josephus,* who has enlarged and garnished it in the Livian style. Agrippa chose a fit locality for this ornate speech. It was an open court in the vicinity of the Temple. Here stood the Herodian titular king and near by, in gay attire, sat his sister, on a veranda of the Hasmonean palace, where all could see her. She looked sad, she wept; and there are good reasons for believing that her tears were not wholly affected. In spite of all her shortcomings she was a far better woman than her sister Drusilla, who, following the custom of the time, had discarded her husband, married the procurator Felix, and become a pagan. She it was, as we learn from the early Christian records, who sat by the side of her Roman spouse when Paul appeared before him;† and on the celebrated Raphael tapestry, at Dresden and at Hampton Court Palace, her figure, standing out more prom-

---

* Wars, II, 16, 4.

† Acts of the Apostles, XXIV, 24.

inently than the rest, may be seen in all its voluptuousness.

The mention of Berenice in connection with this exhibition is the last we hear of her prior to the winter of 67, when, probably about the month of February, she again figures in history. It was at this time that Vespasian landed at the port of Ptolemaïs. His son Titus followed him from Egypt with two legions, and now it was very apparent that Rome was weaving its meshes of war about ill-fated Judea. All sorts of Asiatic feudatories, accompanied by their auxiliaries, appeared there also, to curry favor with the Roman imperator. Agrippa was present, and among his train was his sister Berenice. She was still an attractive woman, and the tender relations which afterwards existed between her and the destroyer of her people, Titus, who was twelve years her junior, date from this time. Josephus, generally so diffuse, makes no mention whatever of this *liaison*. He had good reasons, of course, for keeping silent. But Tacitus, who was too conscientious to suppress events of historical importance, has recorded the fact of Berenice's presence on this occasion and has also informed us that it was her gold which fed Vespasian's insatiable avarice.* What remains to be told the reader will find in Suetonius.

When Rome needed an emperor in place of the weak Vitellius, the appearance of Tiberius Alexander and his Egyptian troops turned the scale in favor of Vespasian, who, through Berenice's scheming, also secured the assistance of her brother-in-law, the Egyptian prefect. As for young Titus, he was so completely under her control, that Berenice already fancied herself securely installed as empress in the palace of the Cæsars. One year later the proudest hopes of the newly founded Flavian dynasty were realized. Judea had been vanquished; she lay in fetters at her victors' feet. While the gorgeous procession, Vespasian in its midst, moved in triumph up the Via Sacra to the Capitoline *arx*, the brave general,

---

* Historia, II, 81.

the dauntless leader of the Zealots, Simon ben-Gioras, was executed in the Mamertine prison, according to that savage Roman custom which demanded a triumphal sacrifice. And at a window of the imperial palace stood a degenerate daughter of Israel, gazing on the wonderful pageant with a cold, calculating glance—a picture that presents to us one of those contrasts by which the caprice of history is wont to signalize the close of great epochs and civilizations, the downfall of states and nations.

Under the name of friend (*amica*), Berenice led an unworthy life in the great Roman's house for more than ten years. Titus' morbid, capricious taste made him a slave to her fading beauty; he guarded her with argus-eyed jealousy and went so far as to have Cæcina, a Roman of rank, put to death, because he suspected him of being a rival for her favor. Nay, Titus wished to make her his wife; but the Romans frowned at the thought of such an alliance, and finally public opinion compelled him to banish her from Rome.* This happened probably at the time of his elevation to the throne, in the year 79; and though Berenice never became his wife, neither did he marry any one else.

Whither did this childless woman, now fifty-one years of age, wend her way, and how long did she survive her disgrace? Cut off from the moral culture of two great races, all her family ties broken, homeless through the cruel and degrading abuse of her own freedom, she at last found a grave, leaving to the world an illegible epitaph and—though scarcely deserving to be remembered at all—an unlovely, but tragic memory.

---

* Suetonius, Titus, VII.

THE

TALMUDIC AGE.

VII.

MARTHA, DAUGHTER OF BOËTHUS.

How inexpressibly sad is the lot of the unfortunate woman whose story we are about to relate! What could she have done to merit the punishment of being thrown into the very midst of the deadly conflict of the Jewish people? Could she have rightfully claimed all the virtues in woman's golden alphabet,*—and it cannot be denied that she possessed some—living among such cruel men and in such evil times, she would still have been irretrievably lost. Unfortunately, she possessed, besides, the pride of better days, the pride by which noble persons not infrequently hasten their downfall, and which, amid the ruin of empires and sanctuaries, sometimes rises to tragic guilt. She was lacking both in tact

---

* The alphabetically arranged Praise of Woman: Proverbs, XXXI, 10–31.

and graceful submissiveness, when the time
came for her to step down from the height
to which she had attained. Once of the
highest rank, a pampered woman, whose
very name Martha מרתא (that is, ruler)
betokened her imperious pride—is it a wonder that she still imagined herself encircled
by the halo of her past glory. But let us
not condemn her too severely for this feminine weakness.

She was the daughter of Boëthus, a man
otherwise unknown. He must have been
very wealthy, and belonged apparently to
the Sadducean circles. The name Boëthus,
to which the Sadducees were very partial,
seems to have been tainted* with heresy
and to have been shunned in rabbinical
circles. In the Echa Rabbati, a Midrash of

---

* Boëthus and Zadok became, according to Aboth
derabbi Natan, 5, the founders of two sects named after
them, whose creeds deviated from tradition. Hamburger's assertion (*Real-Encyclopædie*, II, 1042), that the
Boëthusians took their name from Simon Boëthus, the
father-in-law of Herod, is, on the other hand, to be dismissed as without foundation.

pretty ancient date,* our heroine is continually mentioned as Miriam, the daughter of Boëthus, a master-baker.† The designation was no doubt chosen intentionally to denote one who had grown rich in the bakery business, as we should say. There can be no question, moreover, as to the identity of the two names.‡ Kayserling's hypothesis,§ which makes her the sister of a queen, of the beautiful Mariamne II, wife of Herod and daughter of the Alexandrian priest Simon ben-Boëthus, is, therefore, untenable. No ancient authority makes the slightest mention of this relationship. Were Kayserling right, she must have married the high-priest Joshua ben-Gamala when a woman

---

* Zunz, *Gottesdienstliche Vorträge*, p. 179.

† Echa Rabbati, 67, Col. 3, 4.

‡ Compare, for example, Jerushalmi, Ketuboth, 5, 13, with Echa Rabbati, *l. c.* It is not to be wondered at that this Midrash (*l. c.*, Col. 4) confounds the baker's daughter with the Mother of the Seven Martyrs (see second sketch). Such transpositions are numerous in the earlier Hagada.

§ *Die jüdischen Frauen*, p. 56.

of more than fourscore years, and the sufferings of the nonagenarian, at the time Jerusalem was reduced to ashes, would hardly have been emphasized as a cause of her *untimely* death. The absurdity involved in the acceptance of this hypothesis is evident.

We give preference to the name Martha, vouched for by the Talmud.* We do not believe we shall go far wrong, if we place the birth of Martha—or Miriam—about the year 30 of the common era. When scarcely more than a child, she was married to a man whose name history has not taken the trouble to record, and who after a short period left her a widow amid serious and stormy conditions of life. Who could this short-lived man have been, who bestowed upon the baker's daughter both his heart and his wealth, and then died to make room

---

* Both Gemaras agree in this appellation : Joma 18a; Jebamoth, 6, 4; 61a; Ketuboth 104a; Sukkah 52b; Gittin 56a; Jerushalmi, Ketuboth, 5, 13; furthermore, Sifra, Deut., 281.

for an ambitious priest, friendly to Rome? We only know this, that he was himself a priest; for a son of Martha, who must have been born during her first marriage, officiated as such. Were it not for a casuistical dilemma, to which reference will be made presently, it is more than probable that nothing at all would have been known of her widowhood.

The priest Joshua or, as Josephus* calls him, Jesus, son of Gamala, was of an age when ambition impels us either to vigorous interference or to diplomatic inactivity, according to the exigencies of the case. When the widow was rich and still attractive, he succeeded in winning her hand. It was in the summer of the year 63, and at that time Rome was represented in Jerusalem by the procurator Albinus. High-priests were successively installed in office amid the greatest tumult, dislodging one another like fleeting, shadowy forms.

---

* Life, 38, 41; Antiquities, XX, 9, 4, 7; Wars, IV, 4, 3; 5, 2.

Agrippa II, titular king and president of the Temple, had this high office at his disposal, and during that year as many as three persons, wearing the insignia of high-priest, followed one another at the altar. After Ananus, who remained in office only three months, came Joshua ben-Damneus, who in a short while was succeeded by Joshua ben-Gamala.* As in the days of the greatest corruption, the dignity was purchasable with money or flattery. This time a woman's fond affection paid the required sum.

Agrippa† needed money, much money, for his buildings and his luxurious mode of living. The priest's wife, but recently married, betook herself to him, followed by her

---

* Josephus, Antiquities, XX, 9, 4.

† According to the Talmud, Jebamoth 61a, Joma 18a, the venal king was Alexander Jannai. But he had been laid in the royal sepulchre 142 years before. Besides, Jannai was himself vested with the office of high-priest. Except as to Halachic matters, the Talmud often contains statements wholly at variance with the facts.

slaves, who dragged after her three *kabs**
filled to the top with *denarii.*† This was the
price which Joshua ben-Gamala paid for the
privilege of being anointed high-priest.
As such he was really forbidden to marry a
widow; but, not being possessed of this
dignity at the time of his marriage, the Law
was modified for him by a rule of casuistry,
and he was permitted to retain his wife.‡

The Talmud§ calls attention to the small,
aristocratic hand of Joshua ben-Gamala.
He certainly had the dainty hand of a priest,
one excellently adapted both for burning
incense and bestowing the blessing. The
couple, it must be admitted, employed their
wealth beneficently and wisely. The two
sacrificial lots, made of boxwood, which
were used on the Day of Atonement, he re-

---

* 1 *kab* = 4 *lugs* = 96 eggs.

† The roman silver *denarius* was equal at that time to about twenty cents of our money.

‡ Jebamoth, 6, 4.

§ Jerushalmi, Joma, 5, 2.

placed with golden ones.* This can hardly be considered an act of extraordinary liberality for such wealthy persons, but tradition gratefully records every worthy deed.

Martha fairly worshipped her husband; she was the happiest of women. Alas, that her joyous days should have ended so soon! On the Day of Atonement she repaired to the Temple, to admire her husband in the splendor of his sacred office and as reader of the Torah. On this occasion the way from her residence to the Temple mount was laid with the costliest carpets.†

But we may pardon this love of ostentation, when we remember the great reform which the new high-priest effected in school affairs—a reform rendered possible, indeed, only by the aid of the noble Martha's gold and good-will. In the earliest times, children were taught at home by their parents. Consequently, orphans and the children of the ignorant received, in many instances,

---

* Joma 37a.

† Echa Rabbati, 67, 3.

no instruction at all. Later, Simon ben-Shetach founded schools in Jerusalem; but the right of admission was restricted to advanced pupils, not less than sixteen or seventeen years of age. Ben-Gamala first recognized the urgent need of making the fountain of learning accessible to all. In every large city a school was established, in which instruction of the young was begun as early as their sixth or seventh year. Posterity has preserved the memory of this exceptional deed in the lofty words of praise: "We owe it to the good high-priest that divine learning in Israel has not fallen into oblivion."*

As already mentioned, Martha had a son by her first marriage,† who, as an ordinary priest, took part in the service in the sanctuary with the other priests. The Talmud speaks in most extravagant terms of his

---

* Baba batra 21a; Samuel Marcus, *Zur Schulpädagogik des Talmud*, p. 15, *et seq.*

† This appears from the fact that he was of the lawful age to officiate as priest.

I

physical strength,* which is the only characteristic that distinguished him from the multitude. After this, no further mention is made of him, and he disappears altogether from the recollections of the time. Probably he lost his young life amid the disturbances of the year 67, in the slaughter of the moderate party by the Zealots.†

When her star was still in the zenith, Martha found herself eclipsed by the maternal happiness of her contemporary, the pious Kamit. What woman, whether the wife of a priest or of any one else, could, according to the then accepted notions, compare with Kamit! She had seven sons, and she had seen them all in the vestments of high-priest.‡ Of course, most of them acted merely in the capacity of substitute high-

---

* Sukkah 52b.

† Such seems to be the conclusion of Josephus, Wars, IV, 5, 2. It is hardly likely that a man of rank, who sympathized with Rome, should have survived this massacre.

‡ Joma 47a ; Jerushalmi, Joma, 1, 1 ; Horajot, 3, 2.

priests, and the honor was not one of long duration; sometimes two elections for a substitute were necessary in one day. Nevertheless, it was the quintessence of maternal happiness in those primitive days to have seven sons who could boast of such a distinction.

But poor Martha's good fortune was destined to come to a speedy end. The lustre of her fleeting glory was wholly obscured by the gloom overshadowing her succeeding years. Her husband was not able to retain his high office longer than a year; after that, Agrippa II found it convenient to name a successor in the person of Mathias ben-Theophilus (64–65).[*] History has not stated the motive for this action, but it may easily be read between the lines. Peaceable mediators like ben-Gamala are out of place in such stormy times; their compromises make them disagreeable to all parties.

Unfortunately for himself, the deposed

---

[*] Josephus, Antiquities, XX, 9, 7.

high-priest retained his influential place in the Sanhedrin. As a friend of Josephus, and a secret sympathizer with Rome,* he incurred the suspicion of all parties, and on that account he was singled out for certain destruction. To add to his evil destiny, he possessed, in no small degree, an eloquence of the kind which, upon the approach of catastrophes, embitters opponents without satisfying adherents.

The Idumean troops, called in by the Zealots, lay encamped before the gates of Jerusalem. Joshua ben-Gamala conjured them in a long harangue, delivered from the walls, to return home to their province.† The issue showed with what little success. On the following night the Idumeans forced their way into the ill-defended capital, and the inhabitants were subjected to all the horrors of military despotism. A horribly cruel judgment was visited upon the moderate party. Ananus and Joshua ben-Gamala

---

* Josephus, Life, 41.

† *Ibid.*, Wars, IV, 4, 3.

were the first of the long array of the slaughtered, and the victors, in their fierce fury, even grudged their mangled corpses the peace of the grave.*

Thus Martha, the pampered daughter of wealth, became a widow before she was thirty-seven years of age. It cannot be said that suffering had softened her disposition. She, who was still a rich woman, turned to the Great Council for the customary widow's pension; and that body, with true Jewish generosity, provided for all her wants, even allowing her two *seäs*† of wine per day, though this was contrary to the law, which did not grant wine to women. Yet these efforts in her behalf fell far short of her expectations, and she swore at the reverend tribunal with an unwomanly outburst of passion: "That may be good enough for your daughters;" she cried, "not, however, for Martha, daughter of Boëthus." The

---

* Josephus, Wars, IV, 5, 2.

‡ 1 *seä* = 24 *lugs*. Hence a respectable quantity, the expression being, of course, hyperbolical.

Rabbis, provident fathers, murmured softly, "Amen! We ask no more for our daughters."* Here—as the greatest poets since Homer and the ablest historians teach us—we have another instance of the coarse realism of life. If we expect to find nothing but what is noble and ideal in the heroes of history and tradition, we may as well lay aside the annals of mankind. There is small choice between the fictions of the poets and the severe candor of truth.

A similar exhibition of coarseness is related of another rich woman of those days, Martha, or Miriam,† the spoiled daughter of the wealthy Nicodemus ben-Gorion. She found herself in the same unhappy predicament, and also flew into a passion because her widow's pension, though quite liberal, was in her eyes insufficient. The extravagant elaboration of this story of Nicodemus'

---

* Jerushalmi, Ketuboth, 5, 13.

† Ketuboth 66b. In Jerushalmi, Ketuboth, 5, 13, she is called Miriam, daughter of Simon ben-Gorion; in Echa Rabbati, 67, 3, Miriam, daughter of Nicodemus.

daughter shows that some of the incidents were copied by tradition from the narrative of the daughter of Boëthus. The end, too, of the former is adapted mythically[*] to the unhappy death of the latter. Turning now from this short digression, let us again direct our attention to the vicissitudes which mark the close of our heroine's career.

The unhappy woman seemed destined to empty sorrow's bitter cup to the very dregs; her arrogance brought upon her the full measure of retribution. The famine in besieged Jerusalem was, day by day, assuming a more and more terrible aspect. On one occasion Martha sent her maid to market. "Buy me some fine flour," she said. The girl came back and reported, "There is no more fine flour, but perhaps I may be able to obtain some sifted."—"Then hurry and get me some of it." The same scene was repeated a number of times. But there was

---

[*] For instance, the picking up of the barleycorns and the circumstance of her being dragged to death by a horse: Ketuboth 66b; Jerushalmi, Ketuboth, 5, 13; Echa Rabbati, 67, 3.

no sifted flour, no bran, no barley, no meal, nor, in fact, anything of the kind in market. Then, in desperation, she went herself in search of something to eat. According to one account, she grew faint, was overcome by illness, and died in the public street, delivered at last from her misery. Another version, however, tells us that she sustained herself a few days longer on sucked figs, nay, on the seeds of grain lodged in the hoofs of horses.*

A whole group of legends clusters about the last moments of this unhappy woman. She is said to have been swept by the tide of the fugitives or captives as far as Acco. Here she was furnished with clothing enough to keep her from entire exposure, for she had lost everything. One writer claims to have seen her, tied by the hair to the tail of a fleet horse, dragged along the road from Jerusalem in the direction of Lydda.† It is much more probable, how-

---

* Gittin 56a ; Jerushalmi, Ketuboth, 5, 13.
† Echa Rabbati, *l. c.*

ever, that her death was caused by insufficient and nauseous food.* Toward the end of her career she realized how powerless her riches were to help her, and the thought greatly embittered her. She packed her money and jewels into a bundle, and threw it contemptuously into the street. "Lie there, paltry trash!" she cried, in her last throes. "Valuable treasure, indeed, that could not even help me to a piece of bread!"†

Thus ended the life of Martha, the rich baker's daughter. While it cannot be denied that she was proud and selfish, and had many other ignoble traits of character besides, yet, on the other hand, she was not without some of the better and more refined characteristics of the Jewish female mind. It almost seems as if this sensitive woman had been designedly selected by the events of her time to illustrate, by her vicissitudes and torments, how a great and highly civil-

---

* Gittin, *l. c.;* Jerushalmi, Ketuboth, *l. c.*

† Gittin, *l. c.*

ized government comes to an end. Rarely, indeed, are the stormy conflicts of an age so faithfully reflected in the convulsive pangs of any individual career; and for this reason we thought it due to the unhappy daughter of Boëthus to present the reader with something more than a bare outline of her life.

VIII.

IMA SHALOM.

THE highly-gifted daughter of Simon ben-Gamliel, Ima Shalom, was born about the year 50 C.E., in time to witness the fast departing splendor of Jerusalem. Her father, the energetic president of the Sanhedrin, was not only a zealous defender of the oral Law, but also a patriot, who, according to an uncontradicted tradition of the age, suffered death for his resistance to Rome. As far as fierce party passions would permit, this noble man figured as a sort of leader during the last days of the Jewish commonwealth; and, before his execution, his family saved themselves from the general ruin by living in happy obscurity, awaiting the return of more peaceful times. Thus the inherited claims to power of the house of Hillel, deriving its descent from David, were preserved, and transmitted to a long line of illustrious patriarchs. At the fall of Jerusalem, Gamliel's son, subsequently known in history as the second of that name, was still young, but he found in Rabbi Jochanan ben-Saccai a trusty friend and adviser. Ima Shalom was several years older than her brother Gamliel. Marrying a distinguished teacher of the Law, Rabbi Eliezer, son of Hyrcanus, she accompanied him to Lydda, whither he had transferred his school; but afterwards they went to Cæsarea. They had several children, whose striking beauty the chronicler deemed worthy of record. This is about all we know of the outer life of the woman who meets us at the threshold of the Talmudic world.*

However, chance and the peculiar character of such scanty information as we have of her disclose certain traits in Ima's character that not only reveal the deeper side of her nature, but also cast a strong light upon the women of those days. Ima was no ordinary woman. Thoroughly imbued with

---

* Nedarim 20a, b.

the culture of the school of Hillel, she was quick, witty, and even had some knowledge of the Law; for so completely had its wisdom impregnated the intellectual atmosphere of her age, that no noble mind could have wholly escaped its influence. But she had nothing of Hillel's gentleness; suffering and the cruelties of war had everywhere changed this characteristic into severity and dogmatism. Whithersoever one might look, rigid views of life prevailed, and its most innocent pleasures were prohibited.

By reason of the paucity of the authorities, and the disconnected style of their narratives, Jewish history of this period must be read between the lines. Because our historians, dominated by their bias for certain details of absorbing interest to themselves, have failed to do this, all existing histories of the Jews need, in part, to be entirely reconstructed. It is not enough to give a history of the Tanaim and Amoraim, an account of the Halachoth, the Midrashim, and the earliest forms of prayer;

no, the Jews were also a nation, with a national existence, as the Bar Cochba insurrection and other events attest; and they had a social life as well, always aglow, to be sure, with the intense ardor of religion. Moreover, the history of the Talmudic age is in no small degree the history of Jewish women—women such as Israel may well be proud of. But the Hebrew sibyl, the queen, even the simple housewife and mother, were forgotten in these evil times, whose austerity impressed itself on all things. Jewish women had now become embittered; the more prominent ones, at least, had caught the harshness engendered by interminable controversies, sopheric prejudices, and sectarian narrowness.

While Ima Shalom was living under the guardianship of her brother, the Nasi, or else while on a visit at his house,* a scoffer at religion one day asked Gamliel one of those impertinent questions which then

---

* The common editions speak of Gamliel's daughter, ברתיה. Perhaps the younger Gamliel's father is meant, the word "Simon" being omitted.

formed the chief subjects of dispute. According to one account, this man was a Jewish Christian כופר of a philosophic bent; another version speaks of him as the emperor—קיסר—himself. But, like "consularis" the word "cæsar" appears to have been used to designate any Roman of rank. "By your own Bible," said the scoffer, "your God is little better than a thief; he stole a rib from the sleeping Adam's body." On hearing these words, Ima Shalom, having obtained her brother's permission to resent the insult, cried out: "Lead me before the Prefect (דיכוס); before the Prefect, I say, at once!"—"What wouldst thou with the Prefect?" returned the scoffer.—"I have been wronged. An impudent man broke into my house last night and carried away some silver vessels, leaving golden ones in their stead!"—"And this thou callest a wrong? Would to heaven, such wrong were done me every day."—"Now, see ye, this was exactly Adam's case; for a worthless rib God gave him a helpmeet."—"But the Deity ought not to do good by stealth."

—" Bring me some meat," replied the clever woman. What she demanded was brought her, and, raw and bloody as it was, she roasted it before her questioner's eyes and begged him to taste it. He turned away in disgust. "Seest thou," she concluded, "Adam would also have been displeased, had he been permitted to witness the creation of the first woman."

The intercourse with Jewish Christians, from whose society cultivated Jews, and especially members of the patriarchal family, could not keep aloof, gave rise to various misunderstandings and differences. An adherent of that sect,—Kayserling[*] calls him a lawyer; according to the Talmud,[†] though this is less probable, he was a philosopher—with the importunity peculiar to sectarians, hung about Ima Shalom, trying to persuade her to institute a suit at law against her brother about a legacy. In passing, I ought to say that the philosopher

---

[*] *Die jüdischen Frauen*, p. 126.
[†] Sabbath 116a, b.

must, of course, have known of the quarrel between Gamliel and his brother-in-law Eliezer; otherwise this incident is not easily understood. To set a trap for this tortuous interpreter of laws, Ima offered him a golden candlestick as a bribe, and he gave her the following opinion: "Your law disinheriting daughters is repealed by a new ordinance, which provides for an equal division of the inheritance between the daughters and sons." By the new law (אורייתא אחריתא) he alluded unmistakably to the Gospel. Gamliel, so the story continues, did not let the matter rest there; he outbid his sister by making the philosopher a present of a Libyan ass. Then the arbitrator reversed his first decision, this time evidently referring to the following passage of the Christian evangelist:* "I came not to destroy the law, but to fulfil it." The lady now scornfully reminded him of the candlestick as a sorry symbol of the legal light that had left her cause in such darkness. "Yes,"

---

* Matthew, V, 18.

said Gamliel, with the somewhat clumsy wit of his day, "my ass alone is to blame for this; he came and upset the candle-stick." This story must have an historical basis, for it appears elsewhere in Hagadic literature.*

Apart from its historical value, however, this incident is important for the further reason that it reveals most clearly the true relation in which brother and sister stood to each other. Honored as Eliezer was, he had made himself disagreeable by his obstinacy and positiveness, and the quarrel between him and Gamliel had now become a serious matter. As president of the Sanhedrin, Gamliel excommunicated his brother-in-law, and, in consequence, the celebrated teacher of Lydda was not only misjudged, but also ostracized, and persecuted in a manner which was uncommon even in those ages of implacable dogmatism. Yet Ima Shalom did not waver for a moment in the fulfilment of her duty. The persecuted man being her husband, she felt for him all the sympathy

---

* Pesikta de Rab Kahana, Section Echa, Jalkut, 2, 258.

of a wife, and harbored a lasting resentment against the rash patriarch. No wonder, then, that she did not scruple to annoy the man who called himself her brother with lawsuits about an inheritance.

The Talmud further relates an incident, which is so entirely out of harmony with the spirit of our age, that it can be conveyed to the reader only in a circuitous way. Convinced as Ima was of her husband's innocence, she was apprehensive lest the prayer of one so deeply wronged might work harm to her brother, and she accordingly made Eliezer promise to omit that part of his morning prayer which reserves blessings for the penitent. One day, however, the Rabbi neglected this caution. "Alas," she cried, "what have you done! Perhaps you have caused my brother's death!" This display of fear was all that remained of her sisterly love. And, indeed, the news of the patriarch's decease is said to have come shortly after.* How callous and unbending were

---

* Baba mezia 19b.

the people of that generation! What faith they reposed in miracles and works! Is it at all strange that, only a few decades later, the insurgent Bar Cochba found most enthusiastic supporters?

The practice of foretelling the death of notorious transgressors accorded well with the mental habits of that restless age. On one occasion a pupil of Eliezer's presumed to give certain decisions on his own account in the master's presence. The rabbi, not a little jealous of his authority and embittered through a life of enforced seclusion, flew into a passion, and predicted the presumptious youth's early death.* At such times, turning to his sensible wife, he would say: "Do you see that man, Ima Shalom? He will surely come to grief." This testifies to a much closer intellectual union between husband and wife than was common in those days; for the Tanaim and Amoraim never took their wives into their confidence on such occasions. As there are two other accounts

---

* Erubin 63a.

of this incident in the Palestinean Talmud,* where the Rabbi figures prominently under the title of "Liezer, the exile," we may be sure that it is based on facts. At Cæsarea, where Eliezer's school was located at this time, he brooked no interference with his authority. While at Jamnia, the patriarch had subjected Eliezer to all manner of humiliating annoyances, excluding him even from the academy; but in North Palestine, where he lived during his banishment, he was his own master, and his disciples, making up in faithfulness what they lost in numbers, clung to the sorely-tried sage with unwavering devotion. And his wife's unfailing love, too, cheered and comforted him. What sweet solace to one in whom humility and self-love were so strangely united! If any officious person thrust himself in his affairs, he would say to his highly-gifted, though somewhat quick-tempered wife—for intellectual women are always quick-tempered—"Take a good look at that man, Ima

---

*Gittin, 1, 2; Shebiit, 6, 1.

Shalom! .He will surely come to grief. Aaron's sons, Nadab and Abihu, were not a whit worse." How significant are these words, when considered in this connection! They give us a glimpse of the domestic life of the great master of the Halacha. A man can hate doubly well, when assisted by a wife who is his intellectual equal.

But it would be a mistake to suppose that Eliezer ben-Hyrcanus was at all partial to strong-minded women; he did not like even the moderate specimen of his day. "As well teach a girl what it is improper for her to know," said the Rabbi, "as instruct her in the Torah."* And when a wealthy lady once asked this son of Aaron—for to judge from the Maccabean name Hyrcanus, he must have belonged to that tribe—a very sensible question concerning some passage of the Scriptures, he rebuffed her in an extremely offensive manner, thereby forfeiting a valuable present which she had intended to give him as a tithe. This incident

---

* Sota 20a.

is authenticated by four similar versions, one of which is to be found in each of the two Gemaras, one in the Midrash, and one in the Tosafist.*

The exiled teacher did not long survive his inexorable antagonist. He passed away in the academy at Cæsarea, surrounded in his last moments by a devoted band of pupils. Neither history nor tradition makes any mention of Ima Shalom in connection with her husband's death. Perhaps she preceded him to the grave; for, as a rule, the later descendants of the house of Hillel were not long-lived.

---

* Jerushalmi, Sota, 3, 4; Joma 66b; Numeri Rabba, 9: Tosafot upon Sota 21b.

IX.

RACHEL, RABBI AKIBA'S WIFE.

Through the medium of poetry, very little of which has any real value, as well as through legendary accounts more or less embellished and distorted, the story of Rachel's life has become a commonplace in readers and chrestomathies, and the subject can only be approached with caution by one who would present it from a critical point of view. However, we can get a good idea of the truly feminine and beautiful traits of Rachel's character from some of the main facts of her history, to which, faithfully preserved as they have been by tradition, we will now give our particular attention.

Very few persons were fortunate enough to save their possessions from the general ruin consequent on the fall of the Holy City; and among these was a certain Kalba Shebua, a wealthy citizen of Jerusalem. When the capital was besieged, he promised to supply the people with a sufficient quantity of corn out of his own resources, even though the siege should last twenty-one years. Among the servants who tended this Crœsus' flocks was one of alleged pagan extraction, a handsome man, of fine physique, past the age of youth, who, on subsequently entering the higher walks of life, became famous in history and science. At this time, however, Akiba ben-Joseph—for such was the shepherd's name—was not on good terms with the learned men of his age. Nay, he even hated the Rabbis and sopherim with all the fierceness that belongs to strong, undisciplined natures. "Could I lay my hands on one of these pupils of the learned," he used to say, "no wild ass would bite him more quickly."* And the very grotesqueness of this hatred seems to have been the means of bringing Akiba to the notice of her who afterwards conferred upon him happiness and renown.

Besides being very rich, Kalba Shebua

---

* Pesachim 49b.

was also the happy possessor of a daughter, who was no other than Rachel herself, and when the noble, high-minded girl heard of the audacious words of her father's ignorant servant,—intercourse was free and easy in that age of simplicity—she went in search of Akiba and took him severely to task. "Pray, what harm have the Chachamim done you?" the girl asked, in surprise. "Does such speech become a Judean?"—"And do the learned behave any better?" was the pointed reply. "Do not they, in their pride, look down upon us as defiled?" This observation was, indeed, founded in fact; the doctors of the Law, full of self-conceit, had drawn a sharp line between themselves. and the masses. To satisfy one's self on this point, it is only necessary to read the hard things which are said of the ignorant in the Talmud.* But, be this as it may, even as they argued they looked more and more deeply into each other's eyes, until at last the generous Rachel asked:

---

* Pesachim 49a, b.

"And if I should give myself to thee for life, wouldst thou, out of love for me, become a pupil of the sages?"* It is scarcely necessary to add that they were married. The incident took place in southwestern Palestine, near the city of Jabne, the seat of the Sanhedrin, whither the leaders of the nation fled after Jerusalem had been laid in ashes. The precise locality is not known. It may have been Bene Berak, an unpretending town, not far from the Mediterranean, where Akiba afterwards established his school. At any rate, Rachel and Akiba were united about the year 80, when the traditions of national life were still fresh in the people's memory. Akiba, as has already been observed, was past the first flush of youth; he had, we are told,† a son by a former marriage.

Through this rash alliance the young couple incurred the unrelenting hatred of Rachel's father. It is the same old story in

---

* Ketuboth 62b, 63a.
† Aboth derebbi Natan, 6.

ancient as in modern times: the course of true love never did run smooth. Cast off and disinherited by Kalba Shebua, they were now thrust upon the cold world, and before many days had gone by were glad enough to secure so much as a pallet of straw on which to lay their heads. But, in spite of all her privations, this opulent Judean's pampered daughter uttered not a word of complaint. On the contrary, when she arose in the morning she would smilingly disentangle the straw from her husband's hair; and he, turning his admiring eyes upon her, would then exclaim: "Oh, had I but the means, how gladly would I adorn thy dark locks with a Jerusalem diadem." Akiba here refers to the golden head-bands stamped with the image of the Holy City in ruins, which were worn by the wealthy Jewesses of that day. This ornament served to express the general longing to repossess that venerated spot, Jerusalem—a fervent longing that gathered fresh intensity each year until, finally venting itself in the Bar Cochba insurrection, it caused the blood of the nation's best men to flow in torrents. But poor as were Akiba and his wife, no one more unfortunate than they ever knocked at their hut in vain; and when their destitution reached the lowest point, the faithful Rachel disposed of her luxuriant braids of hair for a few pieces of gold.* What has been related of this couple's privations is not in the least exaggerated; many similar cases are reported to have occurred in ancient times, and, besides, the facts are corroborated by parallel passages of the Talmud. Most likely the proceeds derived from the sale of Rachel's hair were intended to assist poor Akiba on his journey; for after this dreary honeymoon followed years of separation, which Rachel spent in seclusion, while her husband attended the academies of Eliezer ben-Hyrcanus and Nahum—the greatest teachers of their day—at Lydda and Gimso. Probably he also sojourned for some length of time at Jabne.

---

* Jerush., Sabbath, 6, 1; *ibid.*, Sota, 9, 16.

In these years of utter loneliness and extreme want the poor woman was abused and insulted, and her neighbors sneered at her. One day she was accosted by an old acquaintance of her family, who had known her in happier days. " Wilt thou wait forever for one so entirely unworthy of thy love," said the aged man, " thou whom fate has treated more cruelly than a widow?"* The period of Akiba's absence, as also the number of his pupils, has been grossly exaggerated by tradition; but, however that may be, the hour of meeting came at last: an honored Rabbi, a new teacher in Israel, had returned home at the head of a countless multitude of disciples, and the people gathered in crowds to greet him. A beggar clad in rags also hastened thither, and, on recognizing her husband, fell at his feet in speechless agitation. The pupils wanted to thrust her aside, but the sage interposed. "Nay, let her be," said he, clasping his faithful wife once more to his

---

* Ketuboth 62b, 63a.

breast. "What I am, I never could have become, nor could ye have learned of me what ye did, had it not been for her."

And now this worthy couple's trials were at an end. Kalba Shebua not only forgave them, but, retracting his cruel vow, lavished his wealth and possessions on them. Akiba made the noblest use of his riches, although, in this instance, too, our authorities have been guilty of pardonable exaggeration. He particularly remembered the promise once made to Rachel on their pallet of straw; a golden diadem, exquisitely wrought and ornamented with an image of the Holy City, shone in the handsome woman's hair. When the wife of the patriarch Gamliel II saw this precious ornament, it excited her envy, but she begged for one in vain. "Not every wife," said the Nasi, somewhat ungallantly, "has done for her husband what Rachel did for Akiba."*

Akiba's great admiration for his noble-minded wife is beautifully reflected in some

---

* Jerush., Sabbath 25b.

of his sententious sayings. On one occasion the question, " Who is to be esteemed rich ?" came up for discussion among the students of the Torah. " Whoever possesses a hundred vineyards and just as many acres and servants," said Rabbi Tarphon. " No," spoke the great teacher of Bene Berak, " he only is rich who possesses a sensible, virtuous wife."*

In a very concise and enigmatical way we are informed that the daughter of this illustrious couple, following her mother's example, proved to be just as faithful to her betrothed, the learned Ben Asai, under equally trying circumstances. "As the ewe, so the lamb; the child always takes after its mother,"† said the Rabbis, in speaking of Akiba's daughter, who is nowhere mentioned by name. The fact that this young girl's love affair is shrouded in such mystery points to the period of the persecution of the Jews under Hadrian as the probable

---

* Sabbath 25b.

† Ketuboth 63a.

date of its occurrence—a period of evil and disorder, when the noble Rachel was already dead, and the hour of Akiba's painful martyrdom was rapidly approaching. According to another authority, however, Akiba's son-in-law bore the name of Joshua ben Kapusai,* while Simon ben-Asai, who was something of an enthusiast, remained single.†

The Bible tells us of a Rachel whom Jacob loved so well, that he served her father faithfully, amid many difficulties, for fourteen long years. Here we have the picture of another and a better Rachel, who wore upon her tender neck the yoke of that severest of all severe task-masters—dire want.

---

* Sabbath 147a.
† Sota 4b, Tosafot upon Ketuboth 63a.

X.

BERURIA.

WHO has not heard of Beruria, Rabbi Meir's gifted wife? Ministering faithfully to her husband's wants, devoted to her children, possessed of a soul pure, but cold as the freshly fallen snow, with a nature hardened by the terrible deeds and dangers quite common in her day—combining, in short, all the qualities which we should expect to find in a truly great woman of this memorable epoch, she stands out as a classic figure among the female characters of the Talmudic age. She ought to have had some such biographer as Plutarch to record her virtues and eccentricities. Had this privilege been granted her, she would to-day be mentioned in the same breath with distinguished Romans and other illustrious personages, and her name would be heard in colleges and lecture-rooms. Even as it is, she has, in a measure, won renown;

she is and ever will be the greatest female genius, the real heroine of her century. Within the sphere of a woman's vocation, Beruria could not find an outlet for all the passionate ardor of her richly-endowed nature; it reveals itself in its full beauty only in her faith and religious enthusiasm. In times of cruel persecution, when the Jews were closely watched on the slightest suspicion and scholars had to endure much suffering for their devotion to the Law, she was all the more attached to it. Well versed in Halachic lore, she became a skilful, ready, witty controvertist, and though her brilliant sallies and flashes of wit are often marred by a certain caustic gruffness, natural to that unattractive, militant age, yet we never fail to hear a rich note of feminine tenderness.

When—shortly after the terrible year 135—the brave and distinguished Rabbi Chanina ben-Teradion, so relentlessly persecuted by Hadrian, yielded up his life in the cause of Judaism amid the most exquisite tortures, he left his family destitute and without a protector. The wife of this unfortunate man is said to have shared her husband's martyrdom, while his younger daughter was dragged a captive to Rome; but her life and honor were saved by her brother-in-law, Rabbi Meir, who—so at least we are told*—carried her off secretly. The story of Rabbi Meir's journey to Rome has, however, too romantic a setting to be accepted as historical. In a much more impressive account of the terrible punishments inflicted on the principal victims of Roman revenge we are told that a son of Rabbi Chanina, probably during his father's life-time, came to an untimely and inglorious end, after having followed the career of a licentious adventurer.† We shall have occasion to revert to the melancholy fate of this hapless youth.

Our illustrious heroine, at least during the greater part of her life, was far more fortunate than the rest of her family.

---

* Aboda sara 18a.
† Semachoth, 12.

Through personal charms and mental endowments she won the heart and hand of the renowned Halachist, Rabbi Meir, who then mingled freely with the great Akiba's disciples. As a mere girl,—she was born about the year 100—Beruria attracted the notice of her foremost contemporaries by reason of her masculine vigor of intellect and rare learning. In those days troubles, trials and tribulations made it necessary even for the worthiest women to familiarize themselves with the passwords of the schools. It is true that Christianity was then still in its infancy, but its adherents formed a dreaded sect among the Jews and, as its growing influence gave rise to serious dissension in the social world, the nation's noblest minds had always to be on the alert, ready at a moment's notice with their cues and pungent replies. To which must be added the further fact that the undefined political aspirations of Israel's hot-blooded patriots foreshadowed a desperate struggle against all-powerful Rome. Whatever Beruria had to say about any disputed point of the Halacha not only received the respectful consideration of the learned, but was also taken into account in helping them to arrive at a conclusion. Even the patriarch, Rabbi Judah, once expressed his unqualified approval of some opinion of hers.* The ways and regulations of the academy she knew well, and she would often jestingly whisper to the pupils her experience and advice as to the best method of instruction. Seeing a disciple, in contrast to the Oriental readiness of speech and gesture, poring over his parchments in utter silence, she said to him: "Not thus, my friend, canst thou acquire wisdom. In Samuel II, 23, 5, it is written that the body must aid the activity of the soul."† At times she even quizzed the sages, because of the barriers they had raised to a free intercourse between the sexes. "Which way to Lydda?" inquired Jose the Galilean of her. "You might have saved two

---

* Tosefta, Kelim 8, p. 579, ed. Zuckermandel.
† Erubin 53b, 54a.

words," she replied, "in asking that question; 'Where Lydda?' would have fully answered the purpose. You learned men say, you know, that one ought not to waste words on a woman."*

In her controversies with sectaries and Jewish Christians, whose company no intellectual person could altogether shun, and who by their acrimony proved to be a hostile, disintegrating element in the social life of that time, Beruria showed to better advantage. On one occasion, a Sadducee—this is probably but a euphemism for an adherent of the new religion—aimed a blow at Judaism. "Israel has outlived its usefulness; your own prophet speaks sarcastically of its barrenness," said he, referring to Isaiah LIV, 1. "Not at all," was the pointed reply; "the concluding words of the verse prove the contrary; we lack only such degenerate fellows as yourself, and we are glad of it."† This is the origin of the expres-

---

* Erubin 53b.
† Berachoth 10a.

sion, שפיל לסיפיה דקרא, "Look to the concluding words of the verse!" which afterwards found a place among the pointed sayings of the schools. How gentle, on the other hand, was her remonstrance when her husband, provoked to ungovernable anger by the spiteful conduct of some wicked neighbors, invoked curses on their heads. "Nay, Rabbi," said she, calmly; "we ought to pray God to put an end to the sin, not to the sinner."* But then again, we cannot help feeling shocked at her behavior on the occasion of her brother's tragic death. When this profligate youth was lying on his bier, his mouth filled with stones and his body mutilated by the infuriated men who murdered him, Beruria, we are told, had the heart to step up to the corpse and speak this verse from the book of Proverbs: "Bread of falsehood is pleasant to a man; but afterward his mouth will be filled with gravel-stones."† What an awful exhibition of mental strength, and

---

* Berachoth 10a.

† XX, 17.

how well adapted to that steel-hearted generation!

It is through her abiding faith in God, as evidenced by her conduct at the death of her sons, that Beruria is best known to the world. The episode is so touching, that no apology is needed for repeating it here. One Sabbath afternoon, while Rabbi Meir was lecturing in the Beth-Hamidrash, his two promising sons died suddenly. The afflicted mother had the bodies placed on a bed in an upper chamber, and when her husband returned in the evening received him, to all appearance, with her accustomed tranquillity.

"Where are my sons?" asked the Rabbi.

"I suppose they are still at the academy."

"No; they were not there, I missed them," returned the husband.

"They cannot be far away," said Beruria, handing him the wine-cup and giving him his supper. Then she resumed the conversation.

"Rabbi, some time ago an acquaintance gave me some jewels to keep for him, and now he demands them again. Shall I give them back to him?"

"I am astonished that my wife should ask. Can there be any doubt about the matter?"

"Hardly; and yet I did not care to do even this plain duty without thy consent."

Then, leading the Rabbi in silence to the upper chamber, she withdrew the cloths which covered the remains of her beloved children.

"My sons!" cried the stricken father, his wail echoing through the house. "My sons! Light of my eyes! My teachers and guides!"

"Rabbi, didst thou not say even now that we ought to return to the owner, without complaint, what has been entrusted to our safe-keeping? The Lord gave, the Lord hath taken away, blessed be the name of the Lord!"

Strange to say, this well known story, which has passed into universal literature, is taken from a rather late Hagadic record.*

---

* Midrash Mishle upon Prov., XXXI, 10; Jalkut, 2, 963.

The incident probably happened at Tiberias. Here the great Rabbi took up his abode at the close of the Hadrianic persecution, and with the scanty sums that he earned by making copies of the Torah, much sought after on account of the neatness of the writing, he managed to support his family.

What has just been related of Beruria is the last we hear of her in history. Whether she lived to share her husband's glory to the end of his career, or, if not to the end, for what length of time; whether she accompanied him on his numerous journeys, and whether she was cognizant of the intercourse between Rabbi Meir and the Neo-platonic philosopher Numenios—the same who recognized in Plato the Attic Moses*—are matters which we do not know. From the deep silence of the scanty authorities on these points we must infer that her span of

---

* According to the latest biographer, Adolph Blumenthal (*Rabbi Meir*, Frankfort o. t. M. 1888), Abnimus Hagardi was no other than the cynic Œnomaus of Gadora.

life was not very long. So highly gifted a woman would certainly have manifested her presence by some wise saying, subtle turn of expression, and the like. Besides, had Beruria still been alive at the time of the disagreement between her husband and the patriarch Simon III, her influence as a peacemaker would surely have made itself felt.

The last moments of this great woman's career are enveloped in dismal gloom. The Talmud* says that Rabbi Meir fled from his home to Babylon, and that, according to one of the two accounts of the affair then extant, the act was prompted by some misconduct on Beruria's part. This vague statement the latest Hagada† has elaborated into a story of a very tragic character, which I must mention here because my sketch would not be complete without it. May the evil tale be buried for all time to come, and its awful shadow never again fall

---

* Aboda sara 18b.

† See Rashi upon the passage.

across the path of our illustrious heroine! The great Tana's wife, we are told, was often provoked to anger by the saying that "A woman's heart is fickle,"* and would as often ridicule it. "Do not speak so lightly of the sage's words," said the Rabbi one day, in a tone of reproof; "perhaps you may yourself some day experience their truth." And so it happened. Falling into the trap set for her by the Rabbi, who had persuaded one of his pupils to test her virtue, she was so ashamed and mortified by the exposure that she put an end to her life. Now, in the light of all that we positively know to be true concerning Rabbi Meir and his distinguished wife, the improbability of this occurrence is too obvious for demonstration. Without attempting any critical elucidation, therefore, I shall conclude by simply recording my conviction that this calumny ought no longer to be permitted to tarnish the memory of the pure and noble-minded Beruria.

---

* Kiddushin 80b.

XI.

RABBI MEÏR'S PUPIL.

CHAMTA—the Chamat of the Bible—is a town close by Tiberias, so near, in fact, that subsequently the two cities were consolidated into one district.* Rabbi Meïr's place of residence was, at that time, in the latter city, the seat of the Sanhedrin, and here this great teacher and public educator supported himself on the scanty earnings which his mechanical labors, as a transcriber of the Torah, yielded him.

Rabbi Meïr's activity, however, was not confined exclusively to Tiberias. He delivered learned discourses on the Halacha for students and scholars; while his lectures on the Hagada were designed for the general public, including the women. Through

---

*Jerushalmi, Erubin, 5, 7; Neubauer, *La Géographie du Talmud*, p. 207. Three towns are called by the name of Chamat in the Bible. Our Chamta is identical with the place mentioned in Joshua, XIX, 35.

these ingenious homilies, with which he intermingled all sorts of fables, particularly the favorite fable of the fox,—through the homely wisdom, in fact, which is pleasing to the masses, he became the truly popular man of his time. To judge from their effect, his teachings must have fallen from his lips with passionate, persuasive eloquence. Owing, however, to the unfavorable conditions of the times, no evidence of his creative powers has come down to us, with the exception of the mere remnants of three of his three hundred fables of the fox.*

Circumstances connected with the im-

---

* The faint allusions to the three fables in Sanhedrin 38 b, f, Rashi in his commentary tries to make clearer. Perhaps the age of Rashi still possessed reliable traditions concerning this and other Hagadic allusions and subjects. Hai Gaon, too, in his responses, contained in the Collection of Responses of the Gaonim (Schaare teschuba) carefully examines one of Meïr's fables. He was even then acquainted with the Indian origin of this species of poetry, and very properly refers to the book, *Kalila vedimna*.

portant events of his age often called the amiable sage from home, and on such occasions he was easily persuaded to deliver a lecture in whatever place he happened to sojourn. Sabbath, and especially Friday evening, was the time which he preferred for the popular sermon. It is to be observed that the Friday evening discourse, now so much in vogue, can boast of great antiquity. Rabbi Meïr frequently appeared in Chamta, the little suburb of Tiberias, to instruct the multitude. A large assembly always welcomed him there, among whom was a considerable number of women. Woman has always played some part in the early stages, and even in the later development, of religions. When Israel's first pæan was sung, Miriam led the women's chorus, and probably the verse attributed to her is one of the older parts of that song known to be genuine.*

Rabbi Meïr was the favorite preacher

---

* See my dissertation, *Der Gesang am Meere*, in *The Deborah*, 1885.

among women. He knew how to reach their hearts, how to stir their souls. One of his auditors, a daughter of Chamta, burning with desire for knowledge, came very near losing both her peace of mind and her happiness on account of her zeal. To this story I must now invite your attention. The peculiar incident probably took place about the year 150. No mention is made in this connection, and at this time, of Beruria, the noble wife of the great Tana. Perhaps she was no longer among the living, as such sensitive, patient natures seldom live long.* If she had been present, her prudent words and ready wit would certainly have been heard on that occasion.

In relating this incident, I must, in advance, crave the reader's pardon for referring to some revolting manners which belong to this age, and which exemplify the maxim, "Like country, like custom."

Having returned to Chamta,—a town which has become all but historical through

---

* See the sketch, "Beruria," p. 162.

the event about to be related—the Rabbi occupied his usual place on the platform in the academy.* It was Friday evening (as our authorities expressly state), and the sermon had lasted some time. The lights in the large academy were growing dimmer, but the more faithful among the men and women, in their zeal for learning, persisted in remaining to the end; for the honored teacher had seldom spoken with such charm and enthusiasm. Among those who left the hall last was a woman, who by her soulful attention had early roused the curiosity of those present. She was never absent from these discourses, and her eyes were ever intently fixed upon the preacher's lips, with that deep, fervent expression which gives such rounded, spiritual beauty to the female countenance. We shall call her simply Rabbi Meïr's pupil, for she is not known under any other name, and this seems to

---

* That the sermon was preached in Chamta is clear from Jerushalmi, Sota, 1, 14—certainly the oldest accessible authority. See also A. Blumenthal, *Rabbi Meïr*, p. 124.

have been her usual designation among the people of Chamta.

As she rose to go, she threw an almost mournful glance at the platform; she must have surmised what was in store for her at home. She found her husband in a sulky mood. The light of the Sabbath lamp had gone out; she had neglected woman's chief duty on the Sabbath eve—to fill the lamp with oil. The uncomfortable darkness of the house was an accusation against her. She felt this, and hesitatingly approached her husband. She stammered an apology; but he took no notice of it.

"Where have you been so long?" he cried out harshly, in the gloom.

"I sat and listened to the Darschan," was her reply.

"Is that all?" continued the domestic tyrant, spitefully. "Well then, leave me, and enter my house no more until you have spat the preacher in the face."

Such was the treatment of women in the East; we cannot alter the facts. There was in this speech not only coarse scorn, but also a strong element of anti-religious feeling. "The man was a religious scoffer," says one authority, significantly,* and with these words points out the real truth of the matter. The age of the Antoninuses was strongly tinctured with crude philosophical skepticism. The stoic played the *rôle* of philosopher, and Christianity, though still in its infancy, had already begun to rebel against the mother religion.

Like a weeping outcast, the poor woman left her love-lorn home. She had no child there to detain her; otherwise, perhaps, things would not have come to such a pass. Her neighbors were still sitting outside, chatting at their doors; and as they sat there in groups, strangely agitated by conflicting emotions of pleasure and pain, the stars shed their twinkling light upon them. The outcast soon found shelter in the home which some kind friend offered her, and in this hospitable house she spent three weeks without knowing what to do next. On the

---

* Deut. Rabba, 5.

third Sabbath, however, the neighbors urged her to come to some decision in the matter. "Come with us to the academy," they said, "something must be done to reconcile you again to your husband."

Rabbi Meïr had by this time learned how cruelly the philosophical skeptic had treated his wife; an affair of this kind could not be kept a secret for any length of time in Chamta. "The holy spirit had discovered it to him," as it is expressed in the peculiar language of the time by two of our authorities.* "The spirit of the prophet Elias, whose memory is a blessed influence (Secher letob), appeared unto the Rabbi," remarks the other authority.† This can only mean that some inward illumination helped the sage out of the difficulty; for, when the Jews were in great trouble, they always, following the popular belief, had recourse to the benign "Secher letob."

"A serious affection of the eye has sud-

---

* Jerushalmi, Sota, 1, 4 ; Levit. Rabba, 9.
† Deut. Rabba, 5.

denly come upon me," said the Tana, as he noticed the excited group of women in the hall of learning. "Is there among you women one that understands how to charm away this pain in my eye?"

There was one woman who wanted to withdraw timidly, but her companions pushed her forward.

"Let me alone," she cried, despairingly. "I do not understand the charm; I cannot apply the sympathetic remedy."

"My daughter," said the Rabbi, "come nearer, and try at least what your warm saliva will do,"* and, after she had hesitatingly done his bidding, he said to her, in a gentle tone of voice, "Go home, and say to your husband, 'Not once, as you commanded me, but seven times have I spat in Rabbi Meïr's face.'"

Let no one suppose that the story we

---

* The belief of antiquity in sympathetic remedies need not be treated with a disdainful smile. Our age, too, can boast of its share of them. See Osiander, *Volksarzneimittel*, Hannover, 1865.

have just related is a fiction; on the contrary, it is fully corroborated by three authorities, whose accounts agree in the main. It enables us to catch a glimpse of the life of the women of the second century, and also teaches us something of the manners of that age.

There was at first considerable dissatisfaction among Rabbi Meïr's pupils with the decision to which we have just referred, on the ground that the master had thereby diminished the popular respect for the authority of the Law. But the Rabbi tried to pacify them with the following explanation. "No sacrifice," he said, "can be too great, when the question at issue is the reconciliation of husband and wife; even the holy name of God is blotted out with water* at the trial of the woman suspected of adultery. Do you think the honor of Rabbi Meïr stands higher than that of God?"

---

* Numbers, V, 23.

XII.

RABBI ISHMAEL'S MOTHER.

The scene of our story is laid in Kephar Asis, a town in southeastern Palestine, very near the Idumean frontier.* This region, as we learn from a specific decree to that effect, is not at all fertile.† It was probably without any attraction whatever; and its proximity to the Dead Sea gave it a somewhat dull, melancholy appearance. Nothing but an era of severe oppression could have induced the hero of our story to exchange his beautiful Galilean home for this rock of basalt. In the north there were signs on all sides of a fierce, unequal con-

---

* Kilajim, 6, 4.

† On account of the inferior quality of the Idumean barley, married women *in absentia* in that region were awarded a double ration; Ketuboth, 5, 8; Gemara upon this passage, 64b.

flict, the last effort against mighty Rome; the wildest excitement prevailed everywhere. Here in the south, between these fantastic mountain ridges, nature herself seems to have placed an effectual barrier against all attempted hostilities; it would have taken a leader of the enemy a long time to thread his way to this place.

Ishmael needed such a well-fortified nook as this to carry on his extensive activity in teaching. He possessed all the accomplishments of a leader and a legislator; but he was no warrior, no chivalrous knight. This distinction he allowed without envy to his great and older colleague, Akiba. Ishmael, Elisha's son, was a man of peace, of kindly disposition, of quiet, patient submissiveness to God's will.

It was the beginning of the reign of Hadrian, about the year 120—a stormy period for Palestine. Ishmael had passed a joyless youth; when he was still almost a child, he had been dragged to Rome as a hostage. Here Rabbi Joseph ben-Chanania found him, secured him his liberty, and took him back to the Promised Land.* He was of priestly descent, grandson of a high-priest of the same name, who, according to a plausible tradition, suffered martyrdom during the catastrophe of the year 70.† Several historians have confounded this martyred ancestor with his grandson—a piece of carelessness hardly pardonable.‡ Of thirteen prominent characters of this name, mentioned in the literary history of the Talmud,§ the career of Elisha's son— the subject of this sketch—was, above all others, the most peaceful, if not the happiest. He died, at a good old age, in his well protected home, and in the shadow of

---

* Gittin 58a.

† Aboth derebbi Natan, 38.

‡ See Graetz, *Geschichte der Juden*, IV, 71, and Weiss, *dor vedorschav*. On the other hand, see Frankel, *Darke hamischna*, 106; Jacob Brüll, *Mebo hamischna*, 103f; Hamburger, *Real-Encyclopædie*, II, 526; Braunschweiger, *Die Lehrer der Mischnah*, 161f; also Jost, *Geschichte der Israeliten*, III, 211, who seems to have hit upon the proper distinction.

§ According to Juchasin and Seder hadorot.

the great academy—Tana debe Ishmael—
which he founded and which was the means
of preserving his name to posterity. This
wise man's declining years, thus nobly
spent, were preceded by a career equally as
distinguished and as productive of good
results.

His father Elisha, who, though himself
without any particular claims to distinction,
stood between two celebrities in the line
of descent, lived in Galilee, where Ishmael
also first saw the light of day. The latter,
as already mentioned, removed later to
Kephar Asis, and it seems he never left this
quiet academy town but once, when in common
with the leading Tanaim he helped to
remove the Sanhedrin from Jabne to Uscha.*
This journey was rendered absolutely necessary
by the surging wave of political excitement.
But our Rabbi did not tarry long
amid the tumultuous scenes of western
Palestine. After the legal enactment of the
resolutions of Uscha, he returned to his

---

* Brüll, *l. c.*, 104, after Baba batra 28b.

shelter in the southern part of the Holy Land.

It is not the purpose of these pages to enter further into the details of this great Tana's very long, very active and eventful career as a teacher and judge; for our space is limited, and we are under the necessity of introducing to the reader not only a hero, but also a really remarkable heroine. Do not picture to yourself, however, the youthful form of some charming creature, but rather the sedate figure of a worthy matron; think of a mother loving unto adoration.

Day after day this woman observed the noble qualities of mind that manifested themselves in her son's development; she saw in him the willing hand of brotherly love, the sun of the temple of learning, the light of Israel. Her quiet observation moved her at last to a demonstrative act of love. Who can vie with a mother in genuine tenderness? When the sage came home from the academy, all in perspiration, caused by the intense heat of the sun's rays beating against the rocky clefts of En Gaddi, the dear old woman drew near him in a subservient attitude. She gently removed the sandals from his tired feet; and, before he knew it, his toes were bathed in a refreshing stream that fell from a silver basin. Well anointed and invigorated, he sat down to his domestic meal.

Both as a man and a son, Ishmael ben-Elisha shrank from accepting this homage which his mother paid him; he fought against it, and even, two or three times, prevented it; but when he saw tears in her pleading eyes, he acceded to her wish and again submitted to her humble ministry. So this unselfish quarrel took place daily between them, until, on one occasion, Rabbi Ishmael noticed distinctly how his mother, in hurrying away, brought her lips nigh to the cup, in order to sip therefrom, as though some superhuman being had consecrated the liquid by contact with it. Then in a fit of virtuous anger, he cried out: "No, mother, I cannot permit this to go on any longer!"

The next day there was a full attendance at the meeting hall of Ishmael's academy.

People were moving to and fro, pleading their cases and receiving their verdicts. All at once there ensued an expectant silence, and, with hesitating steps, the veiled figure of a woman approached the judges; the voice appeared familiar, yet no one would trust his ears.

"Give him a sound scolding," shouted the matron, pointing at the accused; "reprove his error—Rabbi Ishmael, the great, the wise. Yes, it is true, my son honors not his mother." With these words she lifted the veil, and with frowning countenance stood in the midst of his disciples.

"Honors not his mother!" was the response of a many-voiced echo, and the members of the academy cast down their eyes in shame.

"How do you mean, woman?" exclaimed the vice-president. "We do not understand you."

"It is as I stated," continued Elisha's widow. "I know what he is to the people, and I would fain honor him as my guest. My gratitude to God and my maternal love impel me to act thus, and I insist upon it as my proper right. But he obstinately and almost cruelly tries to prevent me." She then related the peculiar matter of dispute between the two.

"Let her have her way," said the acting Rabbi to the Tana. "As she asks so persistently, obedience to her command is the true fulfilment of filial duty."* So ended this remarkable trial.

Rabbi Ishmael's family life was not quite so happy in other respects as it was in its filial relation. As a father he was sorely tried, and survived most of his children.† The grateful feelings of the female sex, however, made up as far as possible for these vicissitudes of fortune. His gentleness exercised a special fascination over the souls of noble women, and, perhaps, his mother's tender affection for him owes its explanation in part to this fact. The sage of Kephar Asis never lost an opportunity

---

* Jerushalmi, Pea I, 1 ; Tossafot upon Kiddushin 31b.
† Moed katon 28b.

to extend a helping hand to needy women. He acted as advocate for them in the courts, he provided those about to marry with *trousseaux*, he encouraged matrimony, and had inspiring words of praise for Israel's daughters constantly on his lips.* So, in the austere Talmudic world, this noble teacher stands forth as the real, yea, the practical and better Frauenlob. The famous Minnesinger was, as is known, carried to the grave by the fair daughters of Mayence.† On the other hand, the women of Israel chanted a most affecting dirge upon the death of the son of Elisha, and, when he was consigned to his grave, there rang forth these lofty words of Scripture: "O, daughters of Israel, weep for him, as once ye wept for Saul, who clothed you in scarlet, with beautiful trinkets."‡

---

* Brüll, *l. c.*, 113, after Nedarim 66a.

† I may say here, in passing, that several years ago I found his tombstone, in the cloister of the cathedral at Mayence, in a much neglected condition.

‡ Nedarim, 9, 10, with reference to 2 Samuel I, 24; compare also Tossefta, Nedarim, 5.

XIII.

RABBI JUDAH'S MAID-SERVANT.

THE celebrated editor of the Mishnah, Rabbi Judah the Prince, who lived in a truly royal style at Sepphoris in Galilee, was a most liberal and hospitable man. Not only did scholars and disciples consort at his house without the least restraint or reserve, but persons in all walks of life, men of the highest social standing, even Romans of rank, were seen there, coming and going at pleasure. An establishment of this kind, especially when all are welcome to sit down without ceremony at the host's table, needs a prudent manager of no little experience; and the performance of these duties it was which fell to the lot of the woman,— known to us only under the modest title of Rabbi Judah's maid-servant—whose life it is the purpose of this sketch to narrate briefly. In the quiet academy town where the Nasi lived, this manager of the patriarchal house was looked upon as a very odd character—a sort of living heirloom which, as was customary with noble families, passed by descent from father to son; but to those of us who take delight in tracing lost manners and customs, this servant will appear somewhat in the light of a prodigy.

That Rabbi Judah's housekeeper was an extraordinary woman is conclusively proved by the brief, terse, pointed passages which make mention of her. That she was no myth, but actually existed, is clearly established, not only by the fact that we have various concurrent notices of her, but by the character of these notices as well. It is certain, too, that this maid-servant, who in all likelihood had had entire charge of the patriarchal house during the lifetime of Judah's father, Simon III, was an Israelite, or, if not an Israelite by birth, she must have been converted to Judaism in early youth. Any other supposition is hardly possible; for, astonishing enough in case of a Jewish woman, it is absolutely inconceivable that a pagan could have possessed this servant's knowledge of rabbinical expressions and usages. In that case, too, so remarkable a circumstance would certainly have found a place among the records which have been left us. Moreover, still another consideration fully justifies me in concluding that she must have been a Jewess. We are informed—and the Rabbis approved of the act—that she once passed on some one the sentence of lesser excommunication, known as the Niddui, for the space of three years.* The particulars of this incident are given elsewhere in a concurrent passage, to which I shall have occasion to refer later on.

As to her origin and the other circumstances of her life, they are matters of mere conjecture. I infer from her knowledge of the language of the schools and her acquaintance with the writings pertaining to the Scriptures, that she was advanced in years while Judah held office—older, in fact, than her master, whom she nevertheless survived.

---

* Moed katon 17a.

She appears to have been born about 140, and lived to be at least ninety-two years old;* but so little were her faculties impaired by age that the task of inspecting the viands for the Nasi's table was, as a rule, entrusted to this nonagenarian. Whether she had ever been handsome, whether in the brief spring-time of life she had been endowed with that bloom and stateliness which even menial labors cannot affect, may well be doubted. Persons of her mental acuteness usually have very strongly-marked features, which reflect the struggles of their souls and the changes that take place in their inner life, and which, on that account, detract materially from the mere physical beauty of a woman's countenance. I look into her eyes through the veil of centuries and fancy I can see a lofty spiritual beauty in her face, blended with an unmistakable trace of roguishness and, here and there, an ascetic, almost menacing gravity.

Through many years of service in the

---

* Sabbath 152a.

patriarchal house, Judah's servant became thoroughly familiar with the aims and habits of the patriarchs. After her arduous household duties were over, she might be seen leaning over a gallery in the lecture-room, listening to the debates, or now and then she may have mused dreamily over the pithy passages of a discourse contained in an old parchment. Fortunately, evil habits and rude manners are not the only outward influences which help to mould human nature; it is consoling to know that culture enjoys this privilege in a far greater degree. In the Galilean academy, pervaded as it was by an atmosphere of foreign fervor, scarcely any discrimination was made between the sexes; spiritual light radiated in all directions, and there was a ray for every susceptible soul. Considered in connection with these facts, the ready replies which Judah's clever housekeeper has left to posterity acquire much greater importance than would ordinarily attach to them. Living in a large house, where crowds of people congregated, her sharp tongue was the only weapon on which she could rely to make herself respected; and, subordinate though her position was, it required no little audacity on her part to assert her authority against the *naïve* rudeness of the East, as she had always to be prepared to meet such impertinence and mockery with effective retorts.

In almost one breath this sensible woman once explained the meaning of four separate rabbinical expressions in the presence of the learned. The ingenious, roundabout way in which this was done, and her half playful manner of concealing the act, are matters not without interest for one who would know something of the character of those times; and hence I shall here quote an account of the affair as found in the authorities.

"The question was asked: 'What is the meaning of *serugin* (סרגין)?' Then they heard how the maid-servant said to the students of the Law, 'Why do you come separately into the hall, like chopped-up groups (*serugin*)?'—'What does *chaluglugot* (חלוגלוגות) mean?' was asked next. And the maid-servant upbraided an awkward fellow in the following words, 'You disorderly lout, don't scatter your greens (*chaluglugot*) about in this horrible way!'—'How is the passage of the Scriptures, Proverbs, IV, 8, to be translated?' was the third question. And again they heard the housekeeper's voice. 'Haven't you finished curling (*silsel*) your hair yet?'* she said, lecturing probably some foppish house-servant. Again, those learned in the Law were not quite clear as to the meaning of Isaiah, XIV, 23, by reason of the expression *metate* which occurs in that important verse. With a view of shedding light on the subject, the maid-servant gave the following order to one of the female domestics, 'Take your broom (*tate*) and sweep the house thoroughly.'"†

This servant of the Jewish prince was, as

---

* The common rendering, "Prize it (wisdom) highly," is derived from the literal meaning, *to braid, to treat circumstantially*.

† Rosh hashana 26b; Megilla 18a; Nasir 3a; and, with a slight variation, Jerushalmi, Shebiit, 9, 1; *ibid.*, Megilla, 2, 2.

we see, very exacting in household affairs, and felt herself fully equal to the task imposed on her. Her position was a very responsible one; for it must be remembered that to her care were entrusted the treasures of the patriarchal family, which were said to be far more valuable than those of the Persian King Shabur.* She even had charge of the tables reserved by the patriarch for the numerous pupils who received free board at his house; and, as circumstances or her whims dictated, she would either immediately dismiss the students after the meals were over or invite them to remain a while longer. In such company she adopted the technical language known only to the initiated, and employed exclusively by the Rabbis, who scarcely ever expressed the principal idea literally, but nearly always resorted to symbols and figures of speech. One day, when she wanted the pupils to go, she said, "The siphon (mixing vessel) is already striking against the empty jug;

---

* Hamburger, *Real-Encyclopædie*, II, 448.

hence the eagles (the students) must fly back to their nests." On the other hand, when she desired them to remain seated awhile, she would exclaim, "A second cask is going to be tapped, and see, now the siphon is floating at ease, like a boat on the sea!"* Truly, Homer's much-vaunted servants never attained to this degree of education.

But this servant's display of knowledge, acquired through such artificial means, does not afford me nearly so much pleasure as when I think of her indignant at some impropriety of which she had been a witness, her wrinkled cheeks fairly burning with wrath. One day an elderly man administered a flogging to his adult son in the public highway, before her very eyes. Beside herself with indignation, she immediately denounced what is known as the second excommunication (Schamta) against the rude fellow. As she not only had in charge the treasures of the patriarchal family, but also

---

* Erubin 53b.

exercised the authority and power of punishment vested in the Nasi, she had only to utter the word. "The sentence passed upon him," she said with nice perception, "the churl richly deserved according to the provision of Leviticus, XIX, 14. He has in very truth thrown a stumbling block in the way of the blind; for the punishment inflicted by the old man on his son might have readily encouraged the ill-treated youth to raise his hand in retaliation."*

We take leave of this serving matron amid tragic circumstances, strangely colored by the notions of those times. The Nasi's last hour had come, and he suffered terrible agonies while his soul struggled to free itself from its prison of clay. Knowing that it would be for the dying man's good, the stout-hearted housekeeper—for a wife had long since ceased to preside over that household—hastened up to the roof and, although

---

* Moed katon 17a. The two grades of punishment, "Niddin" and "Schamta," are mentioned indiscriminately.

she had before implored God to restore her master to health, she now offered up the following prayer: "Earth is wrestling with Heaven for this precious soul. Take it, O take it, ye heavenly powers!" We may note here, in passing,—a fact which seems to have escaped most scholars—that Simon bar Kappara's poetic announcement of the sad news of Judah's death was simply plagiarized from this intelligent servant's passionate outburst of feeling. But to continue. While she was up-stairs, a crowd of disciples, assembled beneath the trees in an enclosed court of the patriarchal house, were clamorously imploring Heaven to spare the prince's life. According to a prevailing belief of the times, so long as the sick man heard these impassioned prayers—and as he lay in the upper chamber he could scarcely help hearing them—it was impossible for him to draw his last breath. This belief is no conclusive proof of faith in miracles; the prolongation of life through intense momentary excitement is readily explained on psychological, and perhaps also on physiological grounds. But, however this may be, on the roof stood the maid-servant,—not unlike the nornas and weird sisters born of the gloomy imagination of the North—pale as a ghost, trying in vain to make her voice heard below. Then, seizing a jug all of a sudden, she threw it in the midst of the earnest crowd of suppliants. A dreadful pause ensued and, in the inimitable language of the Talmud, "נח נפשיה" (the soul of Rabbi Judah the Patriarch reposed*).

The age in which our heroine flourished appears to have been especially noteworthy for capable, keen-witted women in menial garb. The maid who had charge of the household of Rabban Gamliel the Elder may be cited as another instance; she devoted a great deal of time to the study of religious subjects, and was well versed in the Law.† But no one, whether mistress or maid, deserves to be mentioned with greater praise than Rabbi Judah's maid-servant.

---

* Ketuboth 104a.

† Nidda 6b.

XIV.

THE MARRIED COUPLE OF SIDON.
AN APOLOGUE.

THE Hagada delights in expatiating upon conjugal happiness in the pleasing form of allegories and ingenious fairy tales. Indeed, very few subjects have so great an attraction for the muse of the Jewish patriarchal period as the tender relation existing between the happily married. While the lyric songs of all other peoples—in fact, throughout almost the entire range of literature—sound the praises of love only in its efflorescence, only in its first transports of joy, often flippantly dismissing it with Anacreontic jests, Judaism, as a rule, not only makes conjugal affection the special object of attention, but also treats it in an earnest, even in a pathetic manner. There is nothing more important in life—this is everywhere insisted upon in the realm of legend—than the sacred family tie; no sacrifice, to judge from the allegorists, is too great to strengthen and promote the peace and harmony of pious couples; even the inexorable authority of the Law will somewhat relax its severity, when the matter of bringing husband and wife into closer union is at stake.

In Sidon, the great seaport town, there lived, as Rabbi Idi used to relate, an excellent married couple, loving each other with one heart. They found the greatest happiness of life in mutual faith and tenderness. Moreover, fortune had otherwise favored them; they were rich, and occupied an honored position in the community. What more could these good people want to complete their felicity? Alas, there is nothing perfect on earth! Even in this paradise of domestic bliss there was a great void. Although married ten years, the worthy couple had never yet heard the sweet ring of a child's voice in their magnificent home. This caused them, who otherwise owed so much to the bounty of fate, the deepest sorrow; it was for him, perhaps, even a greater calamity than for her. For the Law rendered its decision with inexorable severity in those times, and, however lovingly he clung to his fair companion, he knew that a higher power would soon tear him from her side. "Not longer than ten years," says the Talmud, "dare a man continue in childless marriage."* "Continue!" No, the ancient book does not express itself so considerately. The authorities of the second century rather ungallantly designate such a relation‡ as "mere lingering."†

---

* Jebamoth, 6, 6; Gemara on this passage; Jebamoth 64ab.

† ושהה עכרה it is called in the Mishnah, *l. c.*

‡ The law, undoubtedly, soon became obsolete, although Maimonides, *Hilchot ischut*, 15, 7, *Eben haëser*, 154, 10, and others still adhered to it. But the commentary to Eben haëser, *l. c.*, early protests against compulsory divorce. Modern authorities rarely refer to the ordinance at all, and even then their judgments are very lenient. According to Mielziner, *The Jewish Law of Marriage and Divorce*, p. 125, the abrogation is contained in Eben haëser; but I can only find it in the much more recent commentary. Of course, the ordinance, so far at least as it relates to obligatory

Must he thrust her from him, who was dearer to him than life? O bitter torment! And yet, what alternative had he? He was free, it is true, to marry another woman; but the better classes had declared themselves against this form of legal bigamy; it was not considered the proper thing in the society in which he moved.* He postponed his decision from day to day, and all the while was greatly depressed in spirits; want of determination, as we know, is a source of self-torment. Nor did he lack fanatical friends, whose advice caused him great anxiety.

divorce, is in contradiction with nearly all modern statutes. To judge from the words which the Midrash ascribes to Rabbi Simon ben-Jochai, I should conclude, that, even in ancient days, the law was seldom enforced, it being greatly preferred to let the parties use their own option.

* I have on previous occasions adduced proof that, even at that time, polygamy had been reduced to a minimum by public opinion, and among those learned in the Law it was as good as abolished. All the Talmudic teachers probably lived in monogamic union.

In Galilee* there lived in those days Akiba's renowned pupil, Rabbi Simon ben-Jochai, revered by the people as a sort of saint. An ascetic, who had renounced the world and had dwelt in caves for many years, he was rigorous in his treatment of himself, but mild and merciful toward his fellow-men. While this great teacher was, on one occasion, sojourning in Sidon,† the distressed couple summoned up courage enough to betake themselves to the Rabbi and beg his advice. "Rabbi," said the man of Sidon, almost choked with tears, "loose our marriage bond, if you think fit."

"Beware of haste, my friend," said the sage, with quick perception of the situation. "When you celebrated your union, it was at

---

* Graetz, *Geschichte der Juden*, IV, 212. Especially in the cave by the village Kephar Charuba, known for its St. John's bread, where he found protection against the persecution of Hadrian: Sabbath 33b.

† That the author of the Apologue regarded Sidon as the best adapted place for the couple to have met the Rabbi is also Hamburger's opinion: *Real-Encyclopædie*, II, 1132.

a feast; so may also your separation be effected at the festive meal."*

The suggestion was promptly followed, and in a very few days the festive table was set in the elegant mansion,—a rare banquet, in which the choicest and the best was offered in profusion for the delectation of the senses. Yet those who occupied the places of honor in the decorated hall, amid gold and silver dishes, were greatly agitated and felt, every moment, as if their heart-strings must burst. They forced themselves, however, to put on a cheerful countenance before their guests; and, when everything was proceeding most smoothly, the host, with raised cup, said to the fair woman he was so soon to leave: "True, this is the last meal we shall share together; yet you shall not depart from this spot of our happiness without a token of my love. Look

---

* Schir haschirim Rabba, *voce:* "Nagila venismecha bach." This is, it is to be noted, the only source for our Hagada, and is positively unique in point of style. We have attempted to reconstruct it, without altering it in substance.

around you, dearest, among the treasures of this house, and the most precious jewel for which your heart yearns—take it, and return in peace to your father's hearth."

When he ceased speaking, she turned her eyes upon him with a look of deep meaning, but she did not answer; she only asked him again and again to drink, herself mixing and spicing the wine, and drinking his health with irresistible grace.

The guests had taken their leave with thanks; the lights burned low in the festive hall. The master of the house, suddenly overcome by a feeling of heavy drowsiness, had sunk down on a soft ottoman. By his side sat she, who was about to part from him; she watched his breathing, and waited until the wine had done its work. Then, beckoning to her male and female servants, she said to them: "Lift him up with the cushions upon which he sleeps, and carry him to my father's house. Be careful of your burden."

It was past the hour of midnight when the sobered sleeper opened his eyes. A dim light streamed from a silver lamp, and by its faint rays he discovered that he was amid strange surroundings. "Where am I?" he asked, in astonishment.

"In the house of my parents," responded his wife.

"But how did I chance here?" he inquired, in greater amazement.

"How did you chance here?" repeated the shrewd woman. "Why, in strict obedience to your own command. Did you not say to me last evening, 'Take with you the most precious thing for which your heart yearns!' Well, in my eyes, dear husband, of all the things I know on earth *you* are the most precious."

A fervid kiss was his only reply; and then, in inexpressible ecstasy, the reunited pair were clasped in each other's arms. They had found each other again, and now fully realized how strong was the love that bound them together.

The next day the couple of Sidon appeared again before Rabbi Simon ben-Jochai. He had expected them, and divined their happy reunion almost at a glance. He approved their resolve to remain united, and dismissed them with a few words of prayer.

Very little remains to be added to this simple narrative. A few happy seasons rolled quickly by, and at the close of a year the noble Sidonian held a lovely child in her arms. Whether through the prayer of the pious sage, or whether through a miracle of a just Providence, she had realized the two most fondly cherished hopes of womanhood: her happiness was complete.

"And, wherefore," Rabbi Idi closes his account, "wherefore this commonplace story? Learn therefrom, O Israel, an important lesson! This woman received a high reward because she designated her husband as her greatest good on earth. Strive to imitate her, O Jewish heart; always seek God and bide His aid. And remember that if you regard Him as your highest good in the world, and, in the words of the Song of Solomon, will 'be glad and rejoice in Him,'* you will be equally rewarded."

This beautiful apologue early claimed the attention of those versed in legendary lore. Its similarity to the narrative of the faithful wives of Weinsberg is very obvious. The Emperor Conrad III, so the chroniclers inform us,† provoked at the little Suabian town's obstinate resistance to his besieging army, determined to put all the men to the sword, and to permit only the women to leave the town, carrying with them their most precious possessions. Thereupon the wives of Weinsberg hit upon the clever idea of carrying their husbands out of the doomed town on their backs, thus saving the whole population.

---

* Schir haschirim, 1, 4.

† A contemporaneous account vouches for the authenticity of the story : Chronicon reg. S. Pantal. ad 1140. The city was taken on December 21, 1140. Something very similar is said to have happened at the siege of Crema, 1159.

XV.

A GROUP OF XANTHIPPES.

THE soil of Palestine and the similarly tempered soil of Babylon were remarkable for their diversified fertility. Nor was this varied luxuriance limited to the natural products of the earth; the human species also, especially woman, there presented itself under such diverse forms of mental and moral development as are rarely found elsewhere. But the creative forces at work in a given place and time cannot be seen in their proper light, so long as our attention is directed solely to the noble and highly developed characters of the particular epoch; those which are eccentric and abnormal must also, if only for the sake of completeness, be taken into account. We have seen the Talmudic woman in the *rôle* of a model wife and mother, we have seen her as an eloquent teacher and a champion of her faith, as a sufferer, as a sybarite, as a princess, and as a lowly servant; and even in the case of those who moved in the higher walks of life we were struck with certain traits that fully prepared us for a display of the stormiest passions of which a woman's soul is capable.

The annals of the past show that females of the Xanthippe type were not confined to Athens and the household of Socrates, as there was no lack of quarrelsome, refractory scolds in the homes of the Tanaim and Amoraim. Not a little has been said, half in jest and half in earnest, in vindication of the class represented by Xanthippe, and the wife of the Grecian sage herself, quite apart from the philosophic grounds on which Socrates justified his readiness to yield to her, has more than once been defended both by ancient and modern writers. But perhaps such few perverse women of the Talmudic period as are known to history may, with even greater justice, claim indulgence at our hands; for, in speaking of them, the unfavorable conditions under which they lived—the troubled times, the enervating influences of the Eastern climate, the degraded position of the sex, the constant strife between the newly-awakened intellectual desires of the age and the tyranny and baser impulses of men—must never be overlooked. Drawn into this conflict, woman, through her intensely emotional temperament and the life of inactivity to which she had been condemned, was ill fortified against all rude shocks, and it ought not in the least to surprise us to find the most susceptible and gifted women of those days the quickest to lose their dignity and temper.

In high as well as low comedy, from Aristophanes to Cervantes, from Shakespeare to Molière, from Gozzi to Scribe, undue prominence has been given to the character of the shrew, and this circumstance, perhaps, has helped very materially to make a type of her. Authors prefer to emphasize the humorous and grotesque, rather than the tragic aspects of family dissensions, and the *rôle* of Xanthippe is not a thankless one, for the laugh is all on her side. This preference springs primarily from the demands of poetic justice; the weak who succeed in defending themselves *appear*, at least, to deserve their victory, even if they go far beyond the limits of self-defence. And to this must be added another psychological observation in which there is much truth. Abusive and quarrelsome women are not necessarily criminals; on the contrary, in spite of their impetuous temper, their raging and fuming, they are generally pure, faithful and conscientious in the performance of their domestic duties. It was not only in the dungeon where the Athenian sage drank the cup of poison that this observation was made; it was confirmed later, on the banks of the Euphrates and Tigris. But far be it from me to defend the termagant. Though it would be wrong to place her on a level with a Locusta or a Lucrezia Borgia, yet, whether living in Babylon or elsewhere, we must not be too lenient in censuring her for her lack of true womanliness and the many annoyances to be laid at her door.

When Rab, the illustrious teacher of Sura, took leave of his uncle and preceptor, Rabbi Chija,—for these scholars used to confide their sorrows to each other in language so affecting as to bring them vividly before us even after the lapse of sixteen centuries—he said to him: "Heaven defend thee from what Koheleth (Eccles., VII, 26) holds as more bitter than death—an ill-tempered wife."*

This incident occurred probably about the year 219, when Rab was preparing to set out on his important mission to Babylon. He had the best of reasons for making the remark; for his wife, out of sheer perverseness, was in the habit of acting contrary to his most innocent requests. If, for example, he ordered lentils for dinner, she would cook chick-peas; if he wanted chick-peas, he would be sure to get lentils; and over such trifling matrimonial squabbles Rab could work himself into a very unphilosophical passion. Taking these troubles of

---

* Jebamoth 63a.

his father's greatly to heart, Rab's young son hit upon a simple device for smoothing over the difficulty; when delivering his father's directions, he would practise upon his mother the deception of altering their meaning. For instance, if the teacher asked for lentils, the lad would change it to peas. Thus, in a roundabout way, the old man obtained what he wished, and on such occasions he would joyfully remark, "After all, your mother is not so bad. Her better qualities, it seems, are beginning to show themselves."—"Would to Heaven it were so," replied the youth, relating the trick which he played on his mother. "Never do that again!" said the father, in a severe tone of reproof. "It certainly looks as if I were training you to lie, and strongly Jeremiah (IX, 4) warns us against teaching our tongues to speak falsehood."*

And Rabbi Chija, too, had to put up with a great deal of annoyance on account of "her of the house" (רביתהו), as the wife,

---

* Jebamoth 63a.

with idiomatic precision, is called in the Talmud. The Rabbi never returned from a walk without bringing her something; but, never so much as thanking him for his presents, she would hide them under cloths and household utensils and keep them entirely for herself. When Rabbi Chija feelingly complained of this to his great colleague, Rab made no attempt whatever to excuse the lady's conduct; on the contrary, he simply exclaimed with Babylonian bluntness: "Why should you grieve over such trifles? Is it not enough that our wives bring up our children and make moral men of us?"*

The chronicles of the household secrets of Sura, Pumbedita, Sepphoris, Tiberias, etc., of course contain many episodes besides those just related. They are, however, of a far more innocent character, and often the thread of the story is lost amid the varied contents of the Talmud. The reader can hardly have forgotten what has been

---

* Jebamoth 63a.

said of Jalta. She, too, it will be recollected, was something of a shrew. Lady Choma, who belongs to the same class, I mean to treat of presently, as I wish to deal separately with important characters.

XVI.

JALTA.

THE woman of whom I have now to speak —Jalta, the pampered daughter of the Prince of the Captivity,—though in some respects unlike the female characters of the Talmudic age hitherto portrayed, has also many points of resemblance to them. In this Babylonian-Jewish sultana we miss entirely the meekness and gentleness of a Rachel, or even of a Beruria. Not, indeed, that she is lacking in nobility of soul and womanly dignity, the excellent education which she gave her daughters proves the contrary;* but her standard of virtue is one which has in a great measure been formed by foreign influences and belongs, besides, to an essentially different age. Without having the great intellectual powers and learning of a Beruria, or the epigrammatic

---

* Gittin 45a.

wit of an Ima Shalom, she was an educated woman with some degree of mental acuteness; and while there is an unmistakable touch of Oriental sensuality always discernible in her mental perceptions, no one can deny that she had the ability to grasp things in their wide and general relations. This mingling of contradictory traits of character and its effect upon her inner nature are most clearly shown in a well-known saying of hers. I refer to the remark in which she has expressed her surprise, that no privation is in reality imposed upon an Israelite by the Jewish Law, because there is something of a very similar nature permitted for almost everything that is prohibited. For instance, while the blood of animals is forbidden, their livers may be eaten instead; the fat of game supplies the place of the fat of animals in general; for swine's flesh a species of fish, the sturgeon, may be substituted; for the Samaritan woman who must not be taken in marriage, there is the female captive of war, and so on. The only prohibition for which she could think of no equivalent concession was the mixing of meat and milk; but her husband, Rabbi Nachman, knew how to solve even this difficulty.*

Compared with the more prominent women of her time, she may be said to represent the capricious type. In her good and bad qualities alike, she is the coddled child of an age which has retrograded somewhat in moral culture and human sympathy. This beautiful epicure, with her equally strong appetite for intellectual pleasures, one can scarcely picture otherwise than seated in her chair of state, in which, at her husband's command, she would go out even on the Sabbath,† carried about by slaves to whom she is not likely to have been a too gentle mistress. The great Babylonian plateau was the place where her life was spent, Sura being probably her home. Babylon afforded every possible opportunity for the full enjoyment of the material pleasures of

---

* Chulin 119b.

† Beza 25b.

o

life; but it lacked those elevating influences and spiritualizing forces which were associated with Palestine and its ruins. For our knowledge of Babylon, this second home of Judaism, we are wholly dependent on the accounts left us by the Talmudists. They claim to have found the Babylonian Jews in a sadly neglected condition, and take to themselves the sole credit of having made of them a very pious and highly intellectual people. No doubt the truth, as in all exaggerations, lies between the two extremes; but the fact nevertheless remains that, judged from a Jewish point of view, the Babylonian type of women was, on the whole, not attractive.

We can hardly go far wrong in assigning the year 240 as the date of Jalta's birth; for on this assumption she would have been in the bloom of her beauty, with all the hopes of youth before her, when—probably about 260—she married the head of the academy at Nehardea, Rabbi Nachman ben-Jacob. This proud, self-conscious man, born about 235, was himself just then entering on his career, and eagerly accepted the newly-created office of supreme judge which his father-in-law's influence obtained for him. It must not be forgotten that Jalta's father was Abba Mari, whom Graetz,* after a critical examination of the subject, regards as the sixth of the Princes of the Captivity. This name Jalta, which occurs nowhere else in the Talmud, is explained as an abbreviation of Ajalta (אילתא), the hind. To have passed one's youth in the house of the exilarchs, to have had a Resh-Gelutha for one's father, are conditions the full significance of which we of the present day can appreciate only with great difficulty. A woman who enjoyed such advantages was attended by swarms of submissive servants and pliant female slaves, who fanned cool air to their mistress's cheeks and with downcast look obeyed her every beck and call. Here court was held and sentences speedily carried out in a way which could not fail to awe subordinates. Officers of the house, sycophants,

---

* *Geschichte der Juden*, Vol. IV, p. 559.

and clients crowded the halls and entries, and their Oriental obsequiousness was of the most repulsive cast. Where there was so much leisure, some part of it was, of course, devoted to study and reading, and from this source Jalta acquired her wit and shrewdness; but many more hours were spent sitting around sumptuous tables, eating from gold and silver vessels, and on gala days regular levees were held, at which the foremost men of the nation were present. Surrounded by such influences, is it any wonder that Jalta should have come unconsciously to assume the haughty airs of a princess? Certainly not, and her husband wedded one who was not only a true descendant of David, but who had also inherited the ancestral pride of the dynasty to which she belonged. The exilarchate was invested with far too much pomp and splendor by the people of those times, and the exilarchs themselves were so intoxicated with their success, so elated over their good fortune, that they dwindled into insignificance, leaving behind them not one worthy deed to record the fact of their existence. Nor are they the only favorites of fortune whom history has consigned to oblivion.

When the happy thought occurred to Rabbi Nachman to offer Jalta his hand, she was still mourning the loss of her first husband. We are not informed of this man's name, but, whoever he was, it appears that his wedded happiness was of short duration; for, to judge from all the surrounding circumstances, Jalta must have been in her prime at the time of her second marriage. Before she had been many months a widow, in fact while she still carried a mere infant in her arms, Rabbi Nachman's wooing put an end to the life of seclusion she had been leading. She entrusted her babe to the care of a nurse, and, quickly comforted, followed her husband to his home.* At the time of which I am speaking Nehardea had already been destroyed by the victorious Odenatus; but in all likelihood Nachman, who succeeded

---

* Ketuboth 60b.

Samuel, had established a new school at Schekenzib, the quiet city on the Tigris, where the pupils driven from Nehardea had assembled again. The provincialism which characterized life in this rising academy town seems to have had no softening influence whatever on Jalta's temperament. In her new home she was as overbearing as ever, and insisted, above all, upon the utmost deference being paid to her by everybody. She was particularly severe in this respect against the learned, whom she had too often seen humbled in this way under her father's roof.

One day, at dinner, a scene took place in Jalta's own house which set in motion the malicious tongues of Schekenzib, a city notorious for its love of mockery.* Rabbi Ulla, who was present as a guest, omitted, on the strength of some surly Halachic comment, to hand her the wine cup after grace. In a great rage at this conduct on the part of the Rabbi, she jumped up, rushed

---

* Pesachim 112b.

into the cellar, and smashed four hundred jugs of wine to pieces. Her guest tried to conciliate her; but, treating him with contempt,—my pen shrinks from recording evidence which gives us so hideous a picture of these times—she made this vulgar reply: "Those who wander about talk idle nonsense, and the clothes of a beggar are full of vermin."* Such punishment falls upon those who marry princesses and fail to lock their wine-cellars.

But, as other incidents in her life attest, Jalta could be very amiable. While she was still living with her father, a pious sage, Rabbi Amram, having been grossly abused by the supercilious servants, took it so to heart that he became seriously ill. With her own hands the princess prepared for him a medical bath, which was the means of restoring the Rabbi to perfect health.† Speaking generally, Jalta seems to have assumed an attitude of haughtiness

---

* Berachoth 51b.
† Gittin 67b.

principally toward her inferiors. Toward her husband she always conducted herself in a manner becoming a wife, and, although the custom of the age encouraged women of wit to put subtle Halachic queries to their husbands, Rabbi Nachman was never thus annoyed. Had she married a better man,—one less selfish than Nachman, from all accounts, must have been—perhaps her richly endowed nature would have flowered into noblest womanhood.

XVII.

ABAJI'S FOSTER-MOTHER.

THE president of the academy of Pumbedita, Abaji, who belonged to the third generation of the Babylonian Amoraim was a man of brilliant parts; but with all his learning, his versatility, his logic and acumen, and in spite of his gentle disposition and noble character, his career nevertheless exhibits all the shortcomings of the age in which he lived. The conditions of the third and fourth centuries did not favor the growth of new ideas, yet they were all the better adapted to labored displays of wit and the exercise of the synthetic faculties; which explains how this able Amora, whose span of life extended from the year 280 to 338, became the real schoolman of the fourth century. The few data which furnish us with the facts of his personal history contain no information as to his origin. As in the case of so many other men of marked intellecual power, poverty was his first teacher. He never knew a parent's love; his mother died in giving him life, while his father had preceded her to the grave.*

What would have become of the talented child, had it not been for the very estimable woman who, qualified in every way to assume the duties of a moral guide, filled the place made vacant by Abaji's parents? History, as sometimes happens, has passed over the name of this worthy foster-mother in silence, nor is the faintest light shed upon the relation in which she stood to Abaji. Whether she took charge of the infant orphan because she was a near relative, or whether the act was prompted by motives of love and mercy, are questions which we shall never be able to answer. Through the gratitude of her foster-son, however, she has won a most honorable appellation; in his recollections she is always spoken of simply as "the mother" or "mother dear" (Em אם).

---

* Kuddushin 31b.

"The Em"—we find the words dozens of times in the Talmud—"told me thus and thus." The name of "the Em" has been used to fill up a very noteworthy page in the history of true womanhood, and hence it may well be retained here.

The fact that Abaji, in the period of his greatest activity, speaks of his foster-mother as of one absent,—most likely referring to one who had already departed this life—makes it probable that she was born sometime about the year 250; and, as it is only with age that one acquires her store of experience, it is safe to assign the year 310 as about the date of her death.

What do we know of the Em? On the the whole, very little; yet fully enough to justify the conclusion that, in spite of having been an eccentric person, whose judgment was warped by the superstitions of her age, she was both eminently practical and exceedingly clever—in short, an original type of woman. It was not only for the numerous benefits which she conferred on the learned Abaji that he gratefully remembered his foster-mother; but also for the large fund of popular lore which she bequeathed to him. Of this some is of value, some wholly innocent, while most of it is colored by the prejudices and necromantic tendency of those times. From all appearances the Em must have enjoyed an enviable reputation as a physician. But she was something more; she was familiar with almost every kind of medicinal herb; her stock of household remedies was inexhaustible—in fact, she controlled the popular medicine of her time in all its branches; and she was, besides, well versed in the theurgy and oneiromancy of those days. Nor were these the only subjects of which she had any knowledge. She had very sound views on matters of education, her occasional quotations of the Halacha were quite correct, and she understood human nature, displaying good judgment in all the affairs of life. "The Em said so," is an expression of which the keen-witted president of Pumbedita often makes use; for he always entertained the highest respect for authority.

The foster-mother's recipes form an important contribution to the popular materia medica of the Talmud, and at the same time bear witness to the faith which the people reposed not only in talismanic influences, but also in magic and supernatural agents. The Em professed to be able to cure all imaginable bodily ills, having on hand the queerest compounds for fainting spells, hemorrhages, fever, melancholia, dyspepsia, and especially for children's diseases. Of course, if she had carried these secrets to the grave with her, humanity would be none the worse off to-day; nevertheless, as serving to throw some light on the character of the times, her peculiar remedies are not without interest. It will not be necessary, however, to cite many of them. Some of them are extremely odd, not to say very repulsive; and the modern reader will be fully satisfied with but a few specimens.

For pains in the chest and stomach, for

instance, she prescribes roasted grains of corn, which is also her cure for low spirits.* Against dyspepsia, perhaps heart diseases also, she recommends meat from the right flank of a ram, together with the ordure of a heifer gathered in the month of Nissan; or, in case this cannot be obtained, chips from a willow-tree may be substituted. The substance taken must then be ignited, and the meat, having been fried at the fire, is to be eaten and washed down with pure wine.†

The following formula, though apparently much less harmful than the one just given, belongs to the same order of remedies. Referring to what we should to-day probably call the ague, the Em says: "If anybody is troubled with a chill and diurnal fever, take a new sus-coin, go to the salt-spring, take a small quantity of salt, roll it about the piece of money, and then tie the whole firmly around the patient's neck by

---

* Erubin 29b.

† *Ibid.*

a braid of hair."* These examples will suffice to give the reader a general idea of the talismanic remedies resorted to by the people of the third century: and it only remains to add in this connection that our physician was not without her panaceas and nostrums, as we learn from her foster-son. "The Em," says Abaji, with an air of importance, " has recommended to me as a plaster for all possible complaints a mixture of six minas of fat and one mina of wax."†

We must leave it to the medical faculty to determine whether the Em's various dietetic hints and prescriptions disclose any knowledge of the secrets of nature. What, for instance, would the modern practitioner think of the following dictum? "Dates before meals," says the Em, "act on the body as blows of the club on the noble palm-tree; but after a meal they are good for the constitution,

---

* Sabbath 66b.

† *Ibid.*, 133b.

they are to digestion what a bar is to a gate."* It sometimes seems to me that in those days, when professional physicians and the Latin *cuisine* of modern times were unknown, these good old folks paid altogether too much attention to household remedies and preventive measures; but this error of overdoctoring one's self is fully counterbalanced by the error of other ages in being overdosed by medical men, so that in the long run things are equalized.

But to return from this digression. For ear-ache the Em regarded extracts of kidney as a sovereign remedy. "The kidney," she says, "seems to have been created only to cure diseases of the ear."† She knew the value of ablutions, and recommends water —but only when warm—for children.‡ On matters of education, too, she has some happy suggestions to offer. For instance, she gives it as her opinion that "a boy

---

* Ketuboth 10b.

† Aboda sara 28b.

‡ Joma 78b.

ought to be made to study the Bible when he reaches his sixth year, and at ten he ought to begin to learn the Mishnah."* And again, the peculiar rule of the ritual, which requires girls to observe the fast-days at twelve years of age, while boys are granted an additional year, on the ground that girls develop more rapidly, and also because boys are more heavily taxed by having to study the Torah, owes its origin to her.†

And in other respects, too, the Em displayed no little practical wisdom. "Six measures heaped," she once declared, "are more than eight measures scattered."‡ Concerning the talk of gossips she tells us: "Town scandal lasts at the farthest one and a half days."§ To judge from this observation the scandalmongers of Pumbedita must have handled their victims with exceptional tenderness.

---

* Ketuboth 50a.
† *Ibid.*, Rashi's comment.
‡ Moed katon 12a.
§ *Ibid.*, 18b.

P

From the manner in which the learned Abaji communicates these various instances of his foster-mother's wisdom to a circle of wise Amoraim, from the fact that he always quotes her with appreciation and assurance, it is apparent that she was highly esteemed in her day. The good Em is, of course, not the only female family physician and prudent housekeeper known to tradition; but, as none is spoken of in terms of such praise, our collection of prominent women of the Talmudic age would not be complete without her.

XVIII.

THE TWO CHOMAS.

THE two characters, of whom we shall give a brief sketch in the following pages, lived at Sura, in Babylon, the seat of the celebrated academy. Though neighbors, they behaved toward each other in anything but a neighborly manner. They were both called *Choma*, signifying "wall" —a name at that time of frequent occurrence in those countries, something like the German *Walpurga*. Although it is very improbable that these women were at all related to each other, they were very well acquainted—a fact which proved all the worse for them, or at least for the one who was destined to become the victim of the stronger. But it was all the better for Sura's tale-bearers, who regarded the animosity between them as most welcome matter for gossip. Of these two women, one was imposing rather than beautiful.

She had an imperious bearing and irritable disposition. This was Choma the shrew, or the strong-minded. Her father was Rab Chasda, the successful director of the Suranian academy, one of those unusually lucky men, whose prosperity tends to soften their disposition, and makes them very indulgent toward their family. The other was Choma the beautiful, a direct descendant of the Palestinian Patriarchs,—Judah the Prince having been her grandfather.

It was anything but agreeable to the strong-minded Choma that people made such an ado of the other Choma's charms; in fact, envy was plainly visible in her somewhat coarse features. The beautiful Choma, on the other hand, was highly gratified at the praises which could not have failed to reach her ears. "She drank wine and laughed," we are told,—a luxury to which, it would seem, her patriarchal descent entitled her.

Thus passed the girlhood of the two Chomas—a very brief period in the Orient. They both married, each choosing a husband to her own liking; the desire to marry being the most reasonable of all woman's ambitions. One day, about the year 320, as Rami and Raba, her father's most distinguished pupils, were seated at his hospitable board, the reverend Chasda, turning to his daughter, the strong-minded Choma, asked: "Which of the two wouldst thou have for thy husband, child?"—"I will take both,"* was the reply. Surely, a bold jest to fall from a maiden's lips; but the *naïveté* of the East furnishes an excuse for many such indelicate expressions. Besides, it must not be forgotten that this happened in the fourth century, when but little of the simplicity of olden days was any longer to be found on the banks of the Euphrates and the Tigris. Nevertheless, we ought not to challenge fate or make light of the decrees of heaven, for many a wanton mocker has been taken at his word. But, to continue our story, Choma gave her hand to the scholar Rami. Their happiness was, how-

---

* Baba batra 12b.

ever, of short duration. Kayserling assumes*
that they were divorced; but the passage to
which he refers† does not bear him out.
After having spent ten years in widowhood,
she married again and became the far happier wife of Raba, the celebrated teacher of
Machusa.

Let us now see what became of Choma
the beautiful. She, also, married a man of
standing, Rachba of Pumbedita, though he
never attained any eminence as a teacher;
and she, also, met with the misfortune of
losing him. But we shall have more to say
of this later. It is sufficient to remark here
that the girlish dreams of the two rivals had
come to an end. They both turned their
backs on Sura—the most maligned of all
academy towns. From the scanty information at our command we can learn very little
about them during their residence in the
city on the Tigris.

Even a shrew's disposition can be softened

---

* *Die jüdischen Frauen*, p. 128.

† Jebamoth 34b.

by domestic happiness; though, to be sure, whenever occasion offers, she will show herself in her true light, as we shall presently see. The tenderness with which this virago clung to the leader of the Metibta school finds its explanation in the conditions of the times. But she was not only strongly attached to her husband, she even sought to protect him against the dangers of magic and the evil powers of demons with which he was beset in his influential position; and, in her zeal, she resorted to all manner of counter-charms which, according to the current notions, might prove effective. Whilst her husband sat in judgment, she would often let her hand—she had had an opening in the wall made for the purpose—rest as it were in protection upon his head.* Does not this act conceal a deep truth? Is there any better safeguard against the evils of life than the arm of a loving woman?

But, on the other hand, thinking herself privileged to go to this length, Choma would

---

* Berachoth 62a.

again and again meddle in affairs wholly unsuited to women. Because she had an imposing figure and a commanding presence, she imagined herself endowed with intellectual powers equally as imposing. One day a woman—who, to judge from what took place, it is fair to conclude must have belonged to the beautiful Choma's circle of acquaintances—was standing in the court room. The oath was about to be administered to her in some suit at law. From what follows, it seems more than probable that the party to be sworn was an intimate acquaintance of Choma the beautiful. The strong-minded Choma, hearing of the proceeding, suddenly burst into the room and cried to her husband, who was acting as judge: "Will you have *that* woman sworn? Do not believe a word of hers! She is utterly unworthy of belief, I have proof of it." Thereupon Raba swore her opponent; and the poor woman, having lost her suit, left the court abashed, with tears in her eyes.*

---

* Ketuboth 85a.

But let us return to the other Choma, of whom we must not altogether lose sight,—Choma the beautiful. She soon laid aside the widow's veil, marrying a second, and even a third time. After the decease of her first husband, she became the wife of Rabba bar bar Chama's son, Rabbi Isaac, a young scholar, whose early death prevented his attaining celebrity. She then gave her hand in marriage to Abaji, the distinguished director of the academy of Pumbedita, whose acquaintance we have already made as the "Em's" foster-son.* This union appears to have lasted some years longer than either of the previous ones; but in the year 338 Judah the Prince's lovely granddaughter was again left alone in the world. A widow who can find consolation in a second marriage occupies anything but an enviable position in the East; and one who has the hardihood to outlive three husbands the Talmud does not scruple to call by the harsh term of "husband-murderer" (Katlanit).

---

* Jebamoth 64b.

Choma the beautiful was under the necessity of appearing in court before her rival's husband, Raba, to obtain her widow's portion in the customary manner. She secured it without any trouble; but, not content with the sum granted her, she also demanded an allowance out of the public moneys for wine, which, she declared, had always flowed freely at Abaji's table. And so saying, she exposed her pretty arm, which gleamed alabaster-like—so says our authority—through the court room.

It is, by the way, a pet weakness of the Talmud to lay stress "on beautiful arms, gleaming like alabaster." The metaphor is found frequently in the pages of the great work. Perhaps, such *Armseligkeit* was characteristic of the taste of that age.

But to resume. "See," cried the excited widow, using her arm as a measure, "Abaji's wine goblets were *so* high!" Not only did such a speech ill become a woman's lips, but the assertion was of doubtful veracity, as the judge very frankly told her.* At the same time, her bluntness ought not altogether to surprise us. Continual ill-treatment of any class of persons is sure to end in their degradation, and to this rule widows, who were certainly not handled too gently in those days, form no exception. The pious judge left the court in disgust, and returned home in a greatly disturbed state of mind. Questioned by his wife as to the cause of his excitement, he gave her an exact account of the whole affair. Pale with rage and jealousy she forthwith rushed out of the house, straight after her hated enemy, whom she overtook not far distant from the court room. Then suddenly the stillness of the academy town was broken by a shrill voice and the sound of blows. "You have already buried three husbands," screamed the ill-tempered Choma, as her wooden sandal fell heavily on her rival's beautiful shoulders, "and now you are trying to lead my husband astray." Nor did she leave off pursuing

---

* Ketuboth 65a.

her, until her fair victim had reached the outskirts of Machusa. How Choma the beautiful managed to get back to her home in Pumbedita, or what subsequently became of her, history nowhere records. Nor is anything known of the latter days of Choma the strong-minded. Perhaps some of my readers may regard so vulgar an exhibition of temper as unworthy of narration; but, as I said before, we are dealing with a virago in the present sketch. This episode, like others of the kind, gives us a bit of the civilization of two Babylonian towns, and faintly reflects the spirit of the fourth century.

XIX.

WEASEL AND WELL AS WITNESSES.

A MAIDEN, not yet out of her teens, walked, or rather ran, over a green field. Judging from her holiday clothes, and the fresh green bough encircling her pretty head, she must have just come from some rural festival;—perhaps she had hurried away in ill humor from the gay gathering. You could almost see a slight touch of anger quivering about her finely chiselled mouth. It was quite early in the afternoon when, alone and unnoticed, she fled from the circle of dancers; but in Palestine it does not take the sun long to travel on its orbit to the west, and after a brief twilight the landscape is wrapped in total darkness.

Owing to the fatigue of rapid walking over a hilly country in the heat of the day, our fair traveller was almost overcome with thirst. There was no human habitation near, where she might, perhaps, obtain a refreshing draught; and she was still quite a distance from the town, where her parents lived. She had hoped to reach her destination in a short time, but fatigue and thirst had retarded her fleeting steps. Her knees began to fail her, she could hardly proceed further.

Then she noticed, by the dying rays of the sinking sun, one of those wells, which it is the benevolent custom of the East to have dug out for the refreshment of wayfarers. There was a wide, funnel-shaped opening at the top of the well. The girl went down three or four steps to the edge of the shaft, grasped the bucket which she found there, and swung it by a rope into the water below. After the lapse of a few minutes, the vessel reappeared with the refreshing liquid. She sipped it, she drank, and the cool draughts drove the fever from her parched lips. But just as she was about to walk up again, she made a misstep on the slippery edge of the well, and, her garments flying in the air, fell into its yawning depth. The silvery stream murmured and eddied below. But for the gloom she could have seen her image as in a looking-glass. She breathed the damp air but a moment, then her senses left her; she could neither see nor hear anything more.

When she regained consciousness, she discovered that she was held fast by her dress. The helpless girl had been caught, in her fall, by a gnarled tree-root, projecting from a wall of earth. Ought she to praise God for such a rescue? She was still suspended motionless in the gloomy shaft of the well; a watery grave awaited her below, and there was no path, no footway to the top. Then, with all the strength that remained to her, she cried out again and again, "Help! Help! Help for God's sake. I am drowning!"

All of a sudden, the elastic step of a man was heard on the greensward above. The wayfarer comes nearer, he stands still, he listens. "Are you a child of man," he asks, shouting into the well, "or one of Ashmedai's* daughters, a wicked demon created to ensnare the sons of earth? Your voice sounds hollow and ghostlike from below."

"I am the daughter of respectable parents. Oh, if you are capable of pity, save one who is doomed to be buried alive!"

"To judge from your voice, you must be young and sensible, and, if you please me and I find you comely, will you go with me, will you be mine?"

"I will; I will belong to my preserver," cried the trembling girl, "only do not let me languish here any longer."

He threw the rope to her. One hearty pull, then another, and, as the unfortunate prisoner was brought to the top, she breathed the night air joyfully, now that she was sure of her rescue. By the light of the rising moon and the glimmer of the stars, each looked the other in the face—

---

* Ashmedai, the well-known prince of demons of Talmudic legend, probably of Persian origin; Gittin 68 ab; Numeri Rabba, 11; Hamburger, *Real-Encyclopædie*, II, 74, *et seq.*

one, a lovely girl, just blooming into maidenhood; the other, a finely formed, vigorous young man. They seemed as if created for each other.

"You please me, little one, and I will keep my promise; you must keep yours, too!" With these words he threw his arms round her slender form. She did not speak. Her blushes, veiled by the darkness of the night, were her only answer.

Thus they walked along, side by side; he pressed his suit more and more urgently; caressing words and vows of love came with increasing fervor from his lips. But of a sudden she tore herself from him, indignantly. "And who are you?" she asked, almost threateningly. "If you are born of noble parents, respect my forlorn condition. Come to my father's house to-morrow morning, and woo me as it is meet to woo a daughter of Israel. My father and mother, I pledge you, will not refuse you my hand."

"I am not only of respectable parents," he replied, somewhat hurt, "but I belong also to Israel's tribe of priests."

"And were you one of the humblest of the land, I would bind myself for life to my preserver."

"Say that once more, beloved," he said, and added, wantonly, "name the witnesses of this declaration which is to bring me so much joy."

At this instant, a timid weasel, frightened out of its hole, passed by the lovers.

"The witnesses," said the fair one, "are everywhere. The sky is our witness; so is the weasel who has heard us; and the well, out of which you rescued me, shall serve as a third witness of our troth."

"So be it," exclaimed the enamored priest, and a fervid kiss sealed the strange betrothal.

"Yonder is the house of my parents," she said, after a while. "Farewell, dear; be sure to remember your promise."

"Farewell, my beloved," he said, "you may depend upon me." And then they separated, she going one way, and he another.

The young bride waited for her lover a

long time with enduring constancy. Many more rural festivals had been celebrated; the vintagers, too, had held their gay dance in the vineyards; autumn was already here; yet the young priest for whom she longed had not returned. "Oh, he will come yet;" she thought, "to-morrow perhaps, or certainly next week." And she stifled her sobs, and in her maiden pride did not betray even by a look the sorrow that weighed on her heart.

There came, too, many worthy youths, who wooed and supplicated and prayed for the hand of this pretty love-lorn maiden. All these offers she coldly rejected. As she found, however, that more than one suitor would positively not be dismissed, and that their visits and offers continued to be more urgently repeated, she hit upon the idea of pretending to be insane. She ruined and tore her clothes, pulled the torn-off pieces into shreds, and would even occasionally seize a visitor by the sleeve and tear off pieces of his clothing. To crown all, she feigned to be afflicted with epilepsy. Her scheme succeeded. It was spread throughout the whole region that she was insane. "Poor girl!" said the people, "her lover's faithlessness has unsettled her reason." Henceforth she ceased to be molested any longer, and was known by her neighbors as the ever-waiting bride.

But what had become of the recreant bridegroom in the meantime? What, indeed! This question has been asked many times, and in a great variety of forms, in Palestine and other lands. When the young man returned home, he remembered his pleasant adventure for several days with sincere joy, and firmly resolved to redeem his plighted word in a short time. Circumstances, however, unfortunately prevented him from carrying out his intention within the first few days after his arrival; he went about his usual occupations, and the longer he deferred the matter, the more indifferent he became. Priests generally have large families, and in the home of most of his acquaintances handsome, dark-eyed girls, of marriageable age, could be found, who might easily bewitch a young man.

Before he knew it, he was smitten with a fascinating maiden belonging to the priestly tribe, without having dismissed his old love from his mind. The marriage was consummated, and, to crown their happiness, a beautiful boy was born unto them within a year. But alas! how fleeting is human happiness, how easily is a parent's hope shattered! Three months had hardly elapsed, when a malignant weasel one day crept up to the side of the sleeping babe, whom the nurse had left for a moment. It buried its sharp teeth in the child's tender body, and sucked the warm blood from his heart. A few seconds later the parents stood over their lifeless darling, wringing their hands in agony.

Another year rolled by, and the young couple were still mourning the loss of their little son. But soon fortune smiled upon them again, and the enraptured mother held a second boy in her arms. His parents were greatly concerned about him and took every precaution to guard him. But in making his first attempts to walk, he would go out into the open air, and found his way to a neighboring well. While bending over its brink, he tottered and fell in. This time there was no gnarled branch at hand to break the fall, and so he sank to the bottom.

This distressing misfortune was still harder for the wretched parents to bear than the first. Deep as was the wife's anguish, however, a violent feeling of wrath took possession of her: wrath against fate, against something mysteriously hostile, she knew not what to call it, that was inmeshing her life. In this mood she seized her husband by the arm, and drew him to a remote corner of the house; it was long since she had shed any tears, but a cold perspiration was on her brow.

"There is something wrong here," she shouted to him, in shrill tones of fear. "Confess now, some dark secret is surely at the bottom of this. If my children had died natural deaths, from some disease, I should, like many another afflicted mother, have to resign myself to the will of God. But these are, indeed, strange causes of death! Confess now, you certainly know the explanation."

His first impulse was to evade the question and flee from this scene. But with his wife's inexpressible suffering staring him in the face, he dared not conceal the truth any longer. He hesitated, he stammered; he sought for words to express himself. "Yes, God is just," he said, at last, trembling from head to foot. "There is, in truth, a secret at the bottom of this." And he told her the whole story of his faithlessness, without the least concealment. He informed her of what had taken place at the well; he told her of the three witnesses of the betrothal: the starry sky, the stealthily creeping weasel, and the yawning well.

"Now I see it all," said the poor woman, after a long, painful pause. "And it is equally clear to me that we must no longer live together. I have no further right to call myself your wife. Go to the poor, disconsolate girl whom you have forsaken. It is God's will that she should be yours. Go to her, and redress the wrong you have done her. Your pleading, your entreaties are all in vain; we must part." And so saying, she turned away, leaving him to his broodings.

The letter of divorce was written, the wife returned to her father's house, and the penitent priest was now preparing to atone for what he had done. He set out without delay for the town where his betrayed bride dwelt. On his arrival he made the necessary inquiries. The people of the place looked at him with a shrug of the shoulders, and said: "You mean the insane girl, the epileptic, who has all these years been waiting patiently for her bridegroom." But he paid no attention to this; he went at once to the house, made an open confession to the girl's father, and also related minutely what had befallen him since the meeting at the well.

"I alone," he concluded his account, "am to blame for the mental disorder with which your noble daughter is afflicted. But God has turned my heart, and I have come to repair all. Give her to me, and in whatever condition I find her I will honor and cherish her through life."

When the old man saw that the priest was sincere in his determination, he led him without further hesitation to his daughter's apartment. "May you succeed, my son," he said, "in bringing my afflicted child back to reason, but I almost doubt your success."

The love-lorn maiden had become so accustomed to feigning insanity, that she always exhibited its symptoms immediately upon the entrance of any stranger, without even looking up to see who it might be. Deeply moved by her strange conduct, the returned lover watched her for a while, until he saw the girl about to fall to the floor with a wild shriek. Then he caught her up in his arms, apparently in an unconscious condition, and gently laid her upon a couch.

"How is it with the weasel?" he whispered in her ear, "and how with the well, and the starry sky? I, your betrothed, am here; I have come to redeem my promise—made in the presence of three witnesses."

She looked up and saw, kneeling beside her couch, him for whom she had waited so long, for whom she had suffered so much. She rubbed her eyes, she laughed and wept in the same breath, and instantly the deep misery that had so long oppressed her soul and clouded her mind lifted itself like a heavy fog.

"Yes, I have waited long," she said, radiant with joy; " yes, my beloved, I have kept the troth we plighted at the well."

How beautiful she looked at this moment! How the happiness of meeting her beloved again made her pale cheeks glow! Surely, there is no better physician, no more potent rejuvenator, than love and happiness!

At last the bride and bridegroom were happily united, and Rabbi Chanina,[*] who transmits the story, takes occasion to exclaim: "There is true magic power in

---

[*] So the Aruch has it ; but in the older version (Tanit 8a) the name of Rab Ammi appears.

faith. This our noble maiden discovered in her steadfast loyalty toward the two witnesses of her betrothal, the weasel and the well; and this all people experience in even greater degree, whose hope and trust are in the Holy One. For towards the faithful in the land, says the psalmist,* God's eyes are always directed."

From all indications it appears that this story belongs to the Talmudic age, and the scene is undoubtedly laid in Palestine.†

---

* Psalm CI, 6.

† This story is alluded to in an earlier record (Tanit 8a). The Gaonic age, without doubt, possessed a tradition in which this rather obscure allusion to the incidents above narrated is explained; and the oldest Talmudic commentators, to whom this tradition was certainly known, have each added touches to the little romance. Even Rashi, in his commentary, has elucidated the original fragment by a short explanation; while Rabbi Nathan relates the story in great detail in the Aruch, *voce* חולדה. Compare also Levy, Neuhebräisches und chaldäisches Wörterbuch, II, 53.

CONCLUSION.

IN the vari-colored group of thirteen portraits, we have now before us the different types of Jewish women of Talmudic times, covering a period of six centuries. Some of our heroines—as, for instance, Rabbi Akiba's wife, Beruria, Rabbi Meïr's pupil, Rabbi Ishmael's mother—stand forth as noble patterns of womanhood, such as are seldom found among the inspired creations of poetry and then hardly surpassed in sublimity. Others are the product of their age, embodying, so to speak, its distinctive characteristics—what is good in it, and its imperfections and prejudices as well; while there are still others who, struggling to maintain themselves in a revolutionary age, amid many trials and great misfortunes, exhibit all the evil influences of their surroundings. To these fortune showed but little favor; and, as a consequence, they are sadly devoid of all that is noble in woman.

Naturally, then, the portraits in our gallery are not all pictures of saintly or ideal beings. We have endeavored to present, with generous appreciation, the better representatives of womanhood of past times; but we have never concealed, and seldom excused, the exhibitions of extreme rudeness and coarseness for which the unfavorable conditions of those epochs must be held responsible. In our opinion, the peevish, censorious historiographer of the stamp of Antonio—we have reference to the Antonio in Goethe's *Tasso*—often mistakes his calling; and does not accomplish much either in the way of giving us a faithful picture of the past or of quickening enthusiasm for the study of history.

Censure the shortcomings of the Talmudic world as severely as you will, it is, after all, emphatically a world faithful to itself, true in outward appearances, logical in its judgments. This is pre-eminently true of the delineations of female character to be found in the Talmud. Indeed, the abundance of passages of this kind, in the *naïve* forms of expression in which they have, for the most part, been transmitted to us, bear unimpeachable and honorable testimony to the native sense of truth of the rabbinical narrators.

In the continuation of our task, treating of the women of the Middle Ages, we shall —of this we are already conscious—not be so fortunate by far; for the sources of our information are but meagre. We are struck by the manner in which domestic life is thrust in the background by public life; woman does not sufficiently engage the historian's attention; often her career lies hidden beneath a mass of legends. But we will not anticipate. From now on, perhaps for a considerable length of time, our literary aims and purposes shall take us away from the Talmudic world; meanwhile, in submitting these biographical sketches in their present form, we crave the reader's indulgence.

INDEX.

Abaji, Rabbi, ... 233-36, 242, 249
   Foster-mother of, ... 234-41
Abba Mari, Prince, ... 227
Abennerig, ... 85
Abia, ... 92
Absalom, brother of Judah Aristobulus, ... 35
Acra, Queen Helena's Palace in, ... 95
Actium, battle of, ... 63
Adiabne, conversions to Judaism in, ... 86
Adiabenian dynasty's renown in Jerusalem, ... 98
Agrippa II, King of Judea.
   and Berenice, ... 108
   oration in favor of peace by, ... 112
Akiba ben-Joseph, Rabbi, ... 153, 185
   and Rachel, ... 154-59
   daughter of, ... 160
Albinus, ... 125
Alexander, son of Aristobulus, ... 55
Alexandra, daughter of Hyrcanus, ... 55, 65, 77, 81
Alexandra, Salome. (See Salome Alexandra.)
Amram, Rabbi, ... 231
Ananelus, ... 65
Ananias, ... 85, 89
Ananus, ... 126, 132
Antigonus, brother of Judah Aristobulus, ... 32, 61
Antioch as the scene of the Maccabees' fate, . . . 15

272 Index.

Antiochus Epiphanes, King of Syria, ... 15
Antony, Mark, ... 60
Aristobulus, brother of Mariamne, ... 57, 67
    appointed high priest, ... 65
Aristobulus, Judah, son of Hyrcanus, ... 29-34
    and Salome Alexandra, ... 30
Artabanus, Parthian king, ... 90
Assyrians, flight of, ... 7

BABYLONIAN civilization in the fourth century, . . 252
    type of women, ... 226
Bardanes, ... 90
Berenice, daughter of Agrippa I, ... 106-17
    and Agrippa II, ... 108
    and Titus, ... 114-16
    appeal in behalf of the Jews, ... 111
    banished from Rome, ... 119
    marriage to Marcus and Herod, ... 107
Beruria, ... 162-73, 177
    and Rabbi Meïr, ... 168-71, 173
Bethome, battle of, ... 41, 46
Boëthus, ... 122
Byron's poem on Mariamne, ... 81

CÆCINA, ... 116
Castus Gallius, ... 104
Chalcis granted to Herod, ... 107
Chamta = Chamat, Rabbi Meïr's lectures at, ... 176
Chanina ben-Teradion, ... 163
    son of, ... 163
    story of Weasel and Well by, ... 266

Chasda,	244
Chija, Rabbi, and his wife,	221
Choma the Beautiful,	249-51
and Rachba,	246
Choma the Strong-minded,	245
and Raba,	246-48
Chomas, the two,	243-51
Christian Church, reception of Book of Judith by,	13
Christianity, early adherents of,	165
Christians, Jewish, intercourse with,	144, 167
Cleopatra,	62, 63
Cross, alleged death of Antigonus on,	62
death of Pharisees on,	41
Cuspius Fadus,	95
Cypros, mother of Herod,	71
DEMETRIUS,	112
Dio Cassius,	91
Doris, wife of Herod,	58
Drusilla,	109, 113
ELIEZER ben-Hyrcanus,	140, 145-47, 149, 157
Em, the. (See Abaji's Foster-mother.)	
FELIX and Drusilla,	113
Friday evening discourse, Antiquity of,	176
Florus Gestus,	110
GAMLIEL the Elder's maid-servant,	204
Gamliel II, brother of Ima Shalom,	140, 142, 145, 146, 159
Gimso, academy at,	157

R

Graetz, ... 61, 67, 84, 227
Grapte, ... 96
Grotius, Hugo, on the story of Judith, ... 9

HANNAH = Miriam = Martha, daughter of Boëthus, 18
Helena, Queen of Adiabne, ... 84–104
   conversion to Judaism of, ... 87
   life in Palestine, ... 95, 96
   pilgrimage to Jerusalem, ... 94
Herod, King of Judea, ... 57–76, 107
   and Mariamne, ... 58, 61
   claims to gratitude of the Jews of, ... 64
   polygamy introduced by, ... 72
Herodians, misdeeds of, ... 109
High priesthood, sale of, ... 126
Holofernes, ... 5, 7
"Husband-murderer," 249
Hyrcanus, John, ... 29, 57, 94

IDI, Rabbi, story by, ... 206
Idumeans, Victory of, over Judeans, ... 58, 132
Ima Shalom, daughter of Simon ben-Gamliel, . . 139–51
Intellectual union between husband and wife in
   Talmudic times, ... 148
Isaac, Rabbi, son of Rabba bar bar Chama, ... 29
Ishmael, Rabbi, aid to women given by 191
   and his mother, ... 188–91
Izates, King of Adiabne, ... 84–94
   conversion to Judaism of, ... 85
   enthusiasm for Judaism of, ... 89
   tomb of, ... 104

JAEL, ... 11
Jalta, ... 223-32
    and Rabbi Nachman, ... 225, 229, 232
Jason (Joshua) of Cyrene, account of Maccabees by, 16
Jerusalem, longing to repossess, ... 156
    Queen Helena's pilgrimage to, ... 94
Jewish Christians, ... 144, 167
Jews, recourse of, to "Secher letob," 181
Jochanan ben-Saccai, ... 140
Joseph, treasurer of Herod, ... 75
Joseph, uncle of Herod, ... 69, 70, 76
Joseph ben-Chanina, ... 185
Josephus, ... 16, 32-35, 39, 45, 50, 54, 59, 67
                        74, 78, 84, 90, 100, 108, 113
Joshua ben-Damneus, ... 126
Joshua (Jesus) ben-Gamala, ... 37, 124, 126
    and Martha, ... 127-31
    appeal to Zealots by 132
    reform in schools by 129
Joshua ben-Kapusai, ... 161
Judah Aristobulus, ... 29-34
Judah ben-Tabai, ... 52
Judah, Rabbi, the Prince, ... 193, 202, 203
Judaism, maid-servant of, ... 194-204
    and conjugal love, ... 205
    conversions to, ... 49, 86, 87, 92
    influence of, in Adiabne, ... 87
Judeans vanquished, ... 58, 115, 132
Judith, Book of, ... 9, 10
    source of, ... 11, 12

Judith, widow of Menasseh, ...7-12
    as a subject of painters, ... 14
    slaying of Holofernes by, ... 7
Juvenal on Berenice and Agrippa II, ... 108

KAB, a measure, ... 127
Kalba Shebua, ... 152, 159
Kamit and her sons, ... 130
Kayserling, ... 123, 144, 246
Kenedeus, ... 104
Kephar Asis, Rabbi Ishmael at, ... 184, 187
Kinnamus, Parthian king, ... 90

LIEZAR, the Exile. (See Eliezer ben-Hyrcanus.)
Lydda, academy at, ... 157

MACCABEAN AGE as unfavorable to the development of female genius, ... 27
Maccabees, Book of, ... 16, 17, 19
    source of, ... 17
Malichus, ... 57
Marcus, son of Alexander Lysimachus, ... 107, 112
Mariamne, ... 57-81, 109
    and Herod, ... 58, 61
    death of, ... 78
Marriage, Talmudic laws concerning, . . . 37, 207, 249
Martha (= Miriam = Hannah) daughter of Boëthus, 18
                                            37, 122-37
    and Joshua ben-Gemala, ... 125, 128
    stories as to death of, ... 136
Martha (= Miriam) daughter of Nicodemus ben-Gorion, ... 134

Index. 277

Martyrs, the seven,	15
Heroism of mother of,	20
Mathias ben-Theophilus,	131
Mattathias and his five sons,	21
Medical prescriptions of Abaji's foster-mother in the Talmud,	237–41
Meïr, Rabbi,	164, 167, 171, 181, 183
and Beruria,	168–73
as a preacher and teacher,	174–77
pupil of,	178–82
"Miriam and her Sons" (a poem),	22
Metellus Scipio,	55
Middle Ages, Women in the,	270
Monobazus I, King of Adiabne,	84, 87
Monobazus II,	85, 88, 101–103
conversion to Judaism of,	92
Nachman ben-Jacob, Rabbi,	225, 226, 229, 232
Nahum,	157
Nebuchadnezzar, King of Babylonia,	5
Nisibis,	90
Numenios,	71
Obedas,	41
Octavia,	62
Octavius,	63
Ophel, Grapte's building in,	96
Parthian empire,	90
Parthians,	60
Paul,	113
Pausanias,	104

278 Index.

Perea and Syria, conversion to Judaism of pagan
    cities of, ... 149
Pharisees, ... 41-43, 48, 49, 54
    nailing of eight hundred on the cross, ... 41
Plutarch, ... 56
Polemo, of Cilicia, and Berenice, ... 108
Polygamy, revived by Herod, ... 72
    discouraged, ... 208
Pompey, ... 56
Priesthood, high, sale of, ... 126
Ptolemy Soter, ... 41
Pumbedita Academy, ... 233

RAB and his wife, ... 220
Raba, ... 245, 248, 251
Rachba, ... 246
Rachel, daughter of Kalba Shebua, ... 153-61
    and Akiba, ... 154-59
Rami, ... 245
Rome, ... 62, 91

SADDUCEES, ... 43, 44, 48
Salome Alexandra, Queen, = Salominon = Salo-
    mita, ... 28-54
    and Alexander Jannai, ... 35
    and Judah Aristobulus, ... 30
    attitude toward Pharisees of, ... 42-44
    sole ruler of Judea, ... 51
Salome, sister of Herod, ... 86
Sanhedrin, ... 43, 48, 133, 177
Samacha, ... 86

Schekenzib, school at,	230
Schoenfeld, Baruch, poem of, on Miriam,	21
Schools, reforms in,	129
Sennacherib,	11
Seä, a measure,	133
Shrews among Jewish women,	216–22
Sidon, the married couple of,	206–14
Simon bar Kappara's announcement of Judah's death,	203
Simon ben-Asai,	160
Simon ben-Boëthus,	123
Simon ben-Gamliel,	139
Simon ben-Gioras,	116
Simon ben-Jochai,	209, 212, 213
Simon ben-Shetach,	28, 45–48, 51
schools in Jerusalem founded by,	129
Sohemus the Iturean,	75
Syria and Perea, conversion to Judaism, of pagan cities of,	49

TACITUS,	91, 114
Talmud:	
beautiful arms referred to in,	250
ignorance referred to in,	154
medical prescriptions of Abaji's foster-mother in,	237–41
Talmudic Law:	
of childless marriage,	207
on marriage of a high priest,	37
on marriage of widows,	249

Talmudic Times:
    intellectual relation of husband and wife in, .   148
    manner of speech in, ... 198
    women in, ... 142, 269
Tana-debe Ishmael, ... 187
Tarphon, Rabbi, ... 160
Theodorus, ... 41
Tiberius, Alexander, ... 98, 99
    apostasy of, ... 101
Titus, ... 105, 108, 114
Trypho, ... 28

Ulla, Rabbi, ... 230

Valerius, Quintus, ... 56
Vespasian, ... 114, 115
Vitellius, ... 115
Vologases, ... 92

Weasel and Well, story of, ... 253–67
Weinsberg, story of faithful wives of, ... 24
Womanhood, patterns of, ... 268, 269
Women, attendance of, at Rabbi Meïr's lectures, . . 176
    Babylonian type of, ... 226
    in ancient Palestine, ... 215
    in Talmudic times, ... 142, 269
    in the Middle Ages, ... 270
    Rabbi Eliezer's opposition to strong-minded, . 150
    Rabbi Ishmael's aid to, ... 192
    treatment of, in ancient times, ... 179
    Xanthippe, as a type of, ... 216–18
Xanthippe, as a type, ... 216–22

www.ingramcontent.com/pod-product-compliance
Lightning Source LLC
Chambersburg PA
CBHW031339230426
43670CB00006B/379